Scriptures
to
Grow On

Scriptures
to
Grow On

a FAMILY HANDBOOK

Scriptures to Grow On: A Family Handbook
©2000 by Discipleship Publications International
One Merrill Street, Woburn, MA 01801

Printed in the United States of America

Editor: Lois Schmitt
Interior Design: Thais Gloor
Cover Design: Chad Crossland

ISBN: 1-57782-142-4

The majority of this material was previously published
by Baker Book House under the title of
A Handbook of Scriptures to Grow On,
edited by Lois Schmitt and Joyce Price.

FOREWORD

Geri and I discovered very early in raising our children that nothing was more important than teaching them the Bible on a consistent, heartfelt basis. We saw that God's word had an amazing effect on their behavior and attitudes. The Scriptures could speak to their hearts and get results in far more powerful ways than our own words and reasoning ever could. We learned that applying the appropriate scriptures in different situations helped our children to think the right thoughts and to do the right things.

As they grew older, we saw the truth of this lesson more powerfully and vividly demonstrated. Now that our children are leaving home and getting married, we are even more thankful for the power of God's word in their lives. Everything good in our family and in our children has come from our reading, discussing and following the Bible together.

The situations we parents encounter in raising our children are innumerable and complex, and we often do not know where to find the appropriate scriptures to address these situations. This excellent book will be an invaluable tool in helping you solve that problem. Whether you have an infant, a toddler, an elementary school-age child, a preteen, a teenager (or any combination thereof!) you will find yourself turning to this volume again and again. And as you do, you will see the power of God's word at work, training and transforming your children every step of the way.

Sam Laing
Lead Evangelist, Triangle Church
Raleigh, North Carolina

CONTENTS

INTRODUCTION

These commandments that I give you today are to be upon your hearts. Impress them on your children. Talk about them when you sit at home and when you walk along the road, when you lie down and when you get up. Tie them as symbols on your hands and bind them on your foreheads. Write them on the doorframes of your houses and on your gates.

Deuteronomy 6:6-9

Moses spoke timeless truth. We need to hear his words today just as much as parents did when he first spoke them. We must first have the scriptures on our own hearts. Then we must impress them on our children.

So, why is this so hard to put into practice? Our children are growing up in the middle of a very real battle for their souls, and we know that Scripture is powerful weaponry and secure protection. But day-to-day family life is chaotic, noisy and perplexing. Sometimes, in the heat of the spiritual battle, we are hard-pressed to take the calm thought and do the careful study necessary to find just the right scripture to attack the enemy or to protect our child.

Most of us have not become proficient in applying scriptural knowledge. Even well-versed Bible students can have difficulty using the Word in a child-centered context. Concordances are limited, and topical studies may not be on target. When a time of family crisis passes without scriptural input, or whenever a child's character is not seen in scriptural light, golden opportunities are missed.

The following chapters are intended to help you make the most of those opportunities. The topical arrangement provides immediate access to scriptures that address issues encountered by children in everyday living. The focus is on Bible verses that relate to behavior, character and attitudes of the heart. Included are topics that relate to children of all ages—even teens.

How to Use the Book

You can use this book in a number of ways:
    a guide for family devotionals
    an outline for parent-child study time
    a handy memory-verse source
    a basis for an expanded study by an older child
    a convenient "pantry" of spiritual food as the need arises

This icon at the end of many sections is a reference to Bible stories, characters or parables that illustrate the topic. Chapters and major topic areas are, for the most part, organized alphabetically. Scriptures within topics are in order of appearance in the Bible. Consult the index in the back of the book to find topics not listed specifically on the Contents page.

Further Suggestions

It is important to use these verses as often as possible in a *positive* way. We should use scriptures to encourage our children's good traits at least as often as we use them to correct or rebuke our children.

It is also helpful to use Biblical language to describe everyday behavior or character. For example, if a child's action is termed "unkind" rather then "not nice," he can more easily connect with a Bible verse that refers to kindness. As parents, we need to use Bible words so that they become familiar to our children. It has become too easy to refer to problems and undesirable traits in psychological terms. How would Jesus see these behaviors? What language would *he* use to describe them?

If we want our children to be interested in learning to use the Word in their lives, we must make sure they see us learning and applying it as well. If they have a memory verse on the refrigerator door, they need to see that we have one there too. (And we should be open to their asking us to recite it.) Our children need to know we also are under God's authority and protection, and that we also have a passion for his Word.

The Five-Minute Breakfast Study

Spending five minutes a day studying with your child can actually be more effective than studying one hour a week. Daily study is our goal for them, and they love the routine. It's amazing how much they learn in such a short time! In the five-minute breakfast study, you combine spiritual and physical food to get their day off to a great start.

This is simple, easy, and fun. Best of all—it's doable! Choose one topic a week and use only the verse or verses you think are appropriate for your child's age and development. A good Monday through Friday outline is patterned on the word "TODAY." Remember that these are *five-minute* studies!

If your topic is humility, your study outline might be as follows:

- **Take the word apart** (Monday) Write out the verse (or verses) and put it (them) on the refrigerator. Then talk about what the word "humility" means.

- **One good example** (Tuesday) Refer to the verse(s), and use a Bible example or a current-day example of a humble (or prideful) person.

- **Discuss** (Wednesday) Refer to the verse(s), and talk about how a prideful or humble person makes God and other people feel.

- **Apply generally** (Thursday) Let your child quote the verse(s) with help, and talk about how we can be humble or prideful in certain situations.

- **You** (Friday) Let your child quote the verse(s). Then help your child to personally apply the week's lessons. The best way to do this without raising defenses is to simply ask questions. For example, "How do you think you are humble? How do you think you are prideful?" Don't make your child answer if he doesn't want to. (This is not an inquisition.) If you have been using the Scriptures, they will soften his heart, and he will find himself thinking about it. This is what you are training him to do!

There is nothing more important than having God's word on our hearts and impressing it on our children's hearts. We can give them piano, tennis and dance lessons. We can take them from place to place and from activity to activity. We can be at every recital, game and match. But, if we fail to impress the word of God on their hearts, we have not given them what they need most in this life...and what they need most for eternity.

Lois Schmitt
Atlanta, 2000

chapter

1

Growing in Attitudes

13

••Attitudes Originate in the Heart ••••••••••••••••••••

Proverbs 4:23
> Above all else, guard your heart,
> for it is the wellspring of life.

Proverbs 14:30
> A heart at peace gives life to the body,
> but envy rots the bones.

Proverbs 16:5
> The LORD detests all the proud of heart.
> Be sure of this: They will not go unpunished.

Proverbs 17:22
> A cheerful heart is good medicine,
> but a crushed spirit dries up the bones.

Proverbs 18:12
> Before his downfall a man's heart is proud,
> but humility comes before honor.

Proverbs 22:11
> He who loves a pure heart and whose speech is gracious
> will have the king for his friend.

Proverbs 27:19
> As water reflects a face,
> so a man's heart reflects the man.

Jeremiah 17:9-10
> The heart is deceitful above all things
> and beyond cure.
> Who can understand it?
> "I the LORD search the heart
> and examine the mind,
> to reward a man according to his conduct,
> according to what his deeds deserve."

Matthew 6:19-21

"Do not store up for yourselves treasures on earth, where moth and rust destroy, and where thieves break in and steal. But store up for yourselves treasures in heaven, where moth and rust do not destroy, and where thieves do not break in and steal. For where your treasure is, there your heart will be also."

Mark 7:20-23

He went on: "What comes out of a man is what makes him 'unclean.' For from within, out of men's hearts, come evil thoughts, sexual immorality, theft, murder, adultery, greed, malice, deceit, lewdness, envy, slander, arrogance and folly. All these evils come from inside and make a man 'unclean.'"

Hebrews 3:12-13

See to it, brothers, that none of you has a sinful, unbelieving heart that turns away from the living God. But encourage one another daily, as long as it is called Today, so that none of you may be hardened by sin's deceitfulness.

·· Good Attitudes: Contentment ····················

Proverbs 17:1

Better a dry crust with peace and quiet
  than a house full of feasting, with strife.

Ecclesiastes 4:6

Better one handful with tranquillity
  than two handfuls with toil
  and chasing after the wind.

1 Timothy 6:6-8

But godliness with contentment is great gain. For we brought nothing into the world, and we can take nothing out of it. But if we have food and clothing, we will be content with that.

Hebrews 13:5

Keep your lives free from the love of money and be content with what you have, because God has said,

"Never will I leave you;
  never will I forsake you."

 (Illustration: Philippians 4:11-12—Paul content with what he had)

·· Good Attitudes: Forgiveness ························

Proverbs 19:11
> A man's wisdom gives him patience;
>   it is to his glory to overlook an offense.

Proverbs 24:29
> Do not say, "I'll do to him as he has done to me;
>   I'll pay that man back for what he did."

Matthew 5:39-41
> "But I tell you, Do not resist an evil person. If someone strikes you on the right cheek, turn to him the other also. And if someone wants to sue you and take your tunic, let him have your cloak as well. If someone forces you to go one mile, go with him two miles."

Matthew 6:12
> "Forgive us our debts,
>   as we also have forgiven our debtors."

Matthew 6:14-15
> "For if you forgive men when they sin against you, your heavenly Father will also forgive you. But if you do not forgive men their sins, your Father will not forgive your sins."

Mark 11:25
> "And when you stand praying, if you hold anything against anyone, forgive him, so that your Father in heaven may forgive you your sins."

Luke 17:3b-4
> "If your brother sins, rebuke him, and if he repents, forgive him. If he sins against you seven times in a day, and seven times comes back to you and says, 'I repent,' forgive him."

Colossians 3:13
> Bear with each other and forgive whatever grievances you may have against one another. Forgive as the Lord forgave you.

 (Illustration: Matthew 18:21-35—Parable of the unmerciful servant)

·· Good Attitudes: Generosity and Sharing ··············

Psalm 112:5
> Good will come to him who is generous and lends freely,
>   who conducts his affairs with justice.

Proverbs 11:16-17

A kindhearted woman gains respect,
    but ruthless men gain only wealth.
A kind man benefits himself,
    but a cruel man brings trouble on himself.

Proverbs 11:24-25

One man gives freely, yet gains even more;
    another withholds unduly, but comes to poverty.
A generous man will prosper;
    he who refreshes others will himself be refreshed.

Proverbs 14:21

He who despises his neighbor sins,
    but blessed is he who is kind to the needy.

Proverbs 14:31

He who oppresses the poor shows contempt
        for their Maker,
    but whoever is kind to the needy honors God.

Proverbs 19:17

He who is kind to the poor lends to the LORD,
    and he will reward him for what he has done.

Proverbs 21:13

If a man shuts his ears to the cry of the poor,
    he too will cry out and not be answered.

Proverbs 22:9

A generous man will himself be blessed,
    for he shares his food with the poor.

Matthew 6:1-4

"Be careful not to do your 'acts of righteousness' before men, to be seen by them. If you do, you will have no reward from your Father in heaven.

"So when you give to the needy, do not announce it with trumpets, as the hypocrites do in the synagogues and on the streets, to be honored by men. I tell you the truth, they have received their reward in full. But when you give to the needy, do not let your left hand know what your right hand is doing, so that your giving may be in secret. Then your Father, who sees what is done in secret, will reward you."

Acts 20:35

"In everything I did, I showed you that by this kind of hard work we must help the weak, remembering the words the Lord Jesus himself said: 'It is more blessed to give than to receive.'"

Romans 12:15

Rejoice with those who rejoice; mourn with those who mourn.

1 Corinthians 13:4

Love is patient, love is kind. It does not envy, it does not boast, it is not proud.

2 Corinthians 9:6–8

Remember this: Whoever sows sparingly will also reap sparingly, and whoever sows generously will also reap generously. Each man should give what he has decided in his heart to give, not reluctantly or under compulsion, for God loves a cheerful giver. And God is able to make all grace abound to you, so that in all things at all times, having all that you need, you will abound in every good work.

Ephesians 4:32

Be kind and compassionate to one another, forgiving each other, just as in Christ God forgave you.

1 Thessalonians 5:15

Make sure that nobody pays back wrong for wrong, but always try to be kind to each other and to everyone else.

1 Timothy 6:18

Command them to do good, to be rich in good deeds, and to be generous and willing to share.

1 Peter 4:9

Offer hospitality to one another without grumbling.

·· Good Attitudes: Helpfulness ·······················

Ecclesiastes 4:10

If one falls down,
    his friend can help him up.
But pity the man who falls
    and has no one to help him up!

Matthew 20:25-28

Jesus called them together and said, "You know that the rulers of the Gentiles lord it over them, and their high officials exercise authority over them. Not so with you. Instead, whoever wants to become great among you must be your servant, and whoever wants to be first must be your slave—just as the Son of Man did not come to be served, but to serve, and to give his life as a ransom for many."

Acts 9:36

In Joppa there was a disciple named...Dorcas, who was always doing good and helping the poor.

Ephesians 4:29

Do not let any unwholesome talk come out of your mouths, but only what is helpful for building others up according to their needs, that it may benefit those who listen.

··Good Attitudes: Honesty ····························

Proverbs 13:11

Dishonest money dwindles away,
      but he who gathers money little by little
            makes it grow.

Proverbs 16:11

Honest scales and balances are from the LORD;
      all the weights in the bag are of his making.

Proverbs 16:13

Kings take pleasure in honest lips;
      they value a man who speaks the truth.

Proverbs 24:26

An honest answer
      is like a kiss on the lips.

Isaiah 33:15-16a

He who walks righteously
      and speaks what is right,
who rejects gain from extortion
      and keeps his hand from accepting bribes,
who stops his ears against plots of murder
      and shuts his eyes against contemplating evil—
this is the man who will dwell on the heights,
      whose refuge will be the mountain fortress.

Colossians 3:22-23

Slaves, obey your earthly masters in everything; and do it, not only when their eye is on you and to win their favor, but with sincerity of heart and reverence for the Lord. Whatever you do, work at it with all your heart, as working for the Lord, not for men.

1 Peter 2:12

Live such good lives among the pagans that, though they accuse you of doing wrong, they may see your good deeds and glorify God on the day he visits us.

 (Illustration: Genesis 42,43—Jacob's sons return the money placed in their sacks)

·· Good Attitudes: Love ································

Proverbs 3:3

Let love and faithfulness never leave you;
      bind them around your neck,
      write them on the tablet of your heart.

Proverbs 15:17

Better a meal of vegetables where there is love
      than a fattened calf with hatred.

Matthew 5:44

"But I tell you: Love your enemies and pray for those who persecute you."

Matthew 5:46

"If you love those who love you, what reward will you get? Are not even the tax collectors doing that?"

John 14:23

Jesus replied, "If anyone loves me, he will obey my teaching. My Father will love him, and we will come to him and make our home with him."

John 15:17

"This is my command: Love each other."

1 Corinthians 13:4-7

Love is patient, love is kind. It does not envy, it does not boast, it is not proud. It is not rude, it is not self-seeking, it is not easily angered, it keeps no record of wrongs. Love does not delight in evil but rejoices with the truth. It always protects, always trusts, always hopes, always perseveres.

2 Corinthians 5:14
For Christ's love compels us because we are convinced that one died for all, and therefore all died.

1 Peter 1:22
Now that you have purified yourselves by obeying the truth so that you have sincere love for your brothers, love one another deeply, from the heart.

1 John 4:19-21
We love because he first loved us. If anyone says, "I love God," yet hates his brother, he is a liar. For anyone who does not love his brother, whom he has seen, cannot love God, whom he has not seen. And he has given us this command: Whoever loves God must also love his brother.

(Illustrations: John 3:16-18—Love of God for man; Philippians 1:1-11—Love of man for man)

••Good Attitudes: Patience •••••••••••••••••••••••••••••

Psalm 37:7
Be still before the LORD and wait patiently for him;
    do not fret when men succeed in their ways,
    when they carry out their wicked schemes.

Proverbs 14:29
A patient man has great understanding,
    but a quick-tempered man displays folly.

Proverbs 15:18
A hot-tempered man stirs up dissension,
    but a patient man calms a quarrel.

Proverbs 16:32
Better a patient man than a warrior,
    a man who controls his temper than
        one who takes a city.

Proverbs 19:11
A man's wisdom gives him patience;
    it is to his glory to overlook an offense.

Proverbs 25:15
Through patience a ruler can be persuaded,
    and a gentle tongue can break a bone.

1 Corinthians 13:4
Love is patient...

James 5:7–8

Be patient, then, brothers, until the Lord's coming. See how the farmer waits for the land to yield its valuable crop and how patient he is for the autumn and spring rains. You too, be patient and stand firm, because the Lord's coming is near.

 (Illustration: Job 1—Job's patience)

•• Good Attitudes: Thankfulness ••••••••••••••••••••••••

Psalm 100:4

Enter his gates with thanksgiving
   and his courts with praise;
   give thanks to him and praise his name.

Psalm 136:1a

Give thanks to the LORD, for he is good.

Romans 1:21

For although they knew God, they neither glorified him as God nor gave thanks to him, but their thinking became futile and their foolish hearts were darkened.

Philippians 4:6

Do not be anxious about anything, but in everything, by prayer and petition, with thanksgiving, present your requests to God.

Colossians 3:17

And whatever you do, whether in word or deed, do it all in the name of the Lord Jesus, giving thanks to God the Father through him.

 (Illustration: Luke 17:11-19—The one thankful leper)

•• Sinful Attitudes: Deceit ••••••••••••••••••••••••••••

Psalm 5:6

You destroy those who tell lies;
   bloodthirsty and deceitful men
   the LORD abhors.

Proverbs 6:14-15

[A scoundrel] who plots evil with deceit in his heart—
   he always stirs up dissension.
Therefore disaster will overtake him in an instant;
   he will suddenly be destroyed—without remedy.

Proverbs 11:1

The LORD abhors dishonest scales,
but accurate weights are his delight.

Proverbs 12:20

There is deceit in the hearts of those who plot evil,
but joy for those who promote peace.

Proverbs 14:8

The wisdom of the prudent is to give thought
to their ways,
but the folly of fools is deception.

Proverbs 15:4

The tongue that brings healing is a tree of life,
but a deceitful tongue crushes the spirit.

Proverbs 26:18-19

Like a madman shooting
firebrands or deadly arrows
is a man who deceives his neighbor
and says, "I was only joking!"

Proverbs 31:30

Charm is deceptive, and beauty is fleeting;
but a woman who fears the LORD is to be praised.

Luke 16:10

"Whoever can be trusted with very little can also be trusted with much, and whoever is dishonest with very little will also be dishonest with much."

1 Corinthians 3:18-19

Do not deceive yourselves. If any one of you thinks he is wise by the standards of this age, he should become a "fool" so that he may become wise. For the wisdom of this world is foolishness in God's sight. As it is written: "He catches the wise in their craftiness."

•• Sinful Attitudes: Envy and Jealousy ••••••••••••••••••

Psalm 37:1-2

Do not fret because of evil men
or be envious of those who do wrong;
for like the grass they will soon wither,
like green plants they will soon die away.

Psalm 49:16–17

Do not be overawed when a man grows rich,
   when the splendor of his house increases;
for he will take nothing with him when he dies,
   his splendor will not descend with him.

Proverbs 3:31–32

Do not envy a violent man
   or choose any of his ways,
for the LORD detests a perverse man
   but takes the upright into his confidence.

Proverbs 14:30

A heart at peace gives life to the body,
   but envy rots the bones.

Proverbs 23:17

Do not let your heart envy sinners,
   but always be zealous for the fear of the LORD.

Proverbs 24:1–2

Do not envy wicked men,
   do not desire their company;
for their hearts plot violence,
   and their lips talk about making trouble.

Proverbs 24:19–20

Do not fret because of evil men
   or be envious of the wicked,
for the evil man has no future hope,
   and the lamp of the wicked will be snuffed out.

Proverbs 27:4

Anger is cruel and fury overwhelming,
   but who can stand before jealousy?

1 Corinthians 13:4

Love is patient, love is kind. It does not envy, it does not
boast, it is not proud.

Galatians 5:26

Let us not become conceited, provoking and envying each
other.

James 3:14–16

But if you harbor bitter envy and selfish ambition in your
hearts, do not boast about it or deny the truth. Such

"wisdom" does not come down from heaven but is earthly, unspiritual, of the devil. For where you have envy and selfish ambition, there you find disorder and every evil practice.

 (Illustration: Genesis 37:1-4—Joseph's brothers envy him)

•• Sinful Attitudes: Hard-heartedness ••••••••••••••••••••

Psalm 1:6

For the LORD watches over the way of the righteous,
but the way of the wicked will perish.

Psalm 10:2-4

In his arrogance the wicked man hunts down the weak,
who are caught in the schemes he devises.
He boasts of the cravings of his heart;
he blesses the greedy and reviles the LORD.
In his pride the wicked does not seek him;
in all his thoughts there is no room for God.

Proverbs 10:24-25

What the wicked dreads will overtake him;
what the righteous desire will be granted.
When the storm has swept by, the wicked are gone,
but the righteous stand firm forever.

Proverbs 11:21

Be sure of this: The wicked will not go unpunished,
but those who are righteous will go free.

Proverbs 15:26

The LORD detests the thoughts of the wicked,
but those of the pure are pleasing to him.

Proverbs 22:5

In the paths of the wicked lie thorns and snares,
but he who guards his soul stays far from them.

Proverbs 24:1-2

Do not envy wicked men,
do not desire their company;
for their hearts plot violence,
and their lips talk about making trouble.

Proverbs 29:16

When the wicked thrive, so does sin,
but the righteous will see their downfall.

Romans 1:18-19

The wrath of God is being revealed from heaven against all the godlessness and wickedness of men who suppress the truth by their wickedness, since what may be known about God is plain to them, because God has made it plain to them.

1 Thessalonians 5:22

Avoid every kind of evil.

1 Timothy 5:24-25

The sins of some men are obvious, reaching the place of judgment ahead of them; the sins of others trail behind them. In the same way, good deeds are obvious, and even those that are not cannot be hidden.

James 4:17

Anyone, then, who knows the good he ought to do and doesn't do it, sins.

·· Sinful Attitudes: Hatred ····························

Proverbs 10:12

Hatred stirs up dissension,
but love covers over all wrongs.

Proverbs 10:18

He who conceals his hatred has lying lips,
and whoever spreads slander is a fool.

Proverbs 15:17

Better a meal of vegetables where there is love
than a fattened calf with hatred.

Matthew 5:43-44

"You have heard that it was said, 'Love your neighbor and hate your enemy.' But I tell you: Love your enemies and pray for those who persecute you."

Matthew 10:22

"All men will hate you because of me, but he who stands firm to the end will be saved."

John 15:18-19

"If the world hates you, keep in mind that it hated me first. If you belonged to the world, it would love you as its own.

As it is, you do not belong to the world, but I have chosen you out of the world. That is why the world hates you."

1 John 2:9-11

Anyone who claims to be in the light but hates his brother is still in the darkness. Whoever loves his brother lives in the light, and there is nothing in him to make him stumble. But whoever hates his brother is in the darkness and walks around in the darkness; he does not know where he is going, because the darkness has blinded him.

1 John 4:20

If anyone says, "I love God," yet hates his brother, he is a liar. For anyone who does not love his brother, whom he has seen, cannot love God, whom he has not seen.

 (Illustration: Jonah—Jonah's hatred for Ninevah)

•• Sinful Attitudes: Pride ••••••••••••••••••••••••••••••••••

Psalm 5:5

The arrogant cannot stand in your presence;
   you hate all who do wrong.

Psalm 12:3-4

May the LORD cut off all flattering lips
   and every boastful tongue
that says, "We will triumph with our tongues;
   we own our lips—who is our master?"

Proverbs 8:13

To fear the LORD is to hate evil;
   I hate pride and arrogance,
   evil behavior and perverse speech.

Proverbs 13:10

Pride only breeds quarrels,
   but wisdom is found in those who take advice.

Proverbs 16:5

The LORD detests all the proud of heart.
   Be sure of this: They will not go unpunished.

Proverbs 16:18

Pride goes before destruction,
   a haughty spirit before a fall.

Proverbs 18:12

> Before his downfall a man's heart is proud,
> but humility comes before honor.

Proverbs 21:24

> The proud and arrogant man—"Mocker" is his name;
> he behaves with overweening pride.

Proverbs 26:12

> Do you see a man wise in his own eyes?
> There is more hope for a fool than for him.

Proverbs 29:23

> A man's pride brings him low,
> but a man of lowly spirit gains honor.

1 Corinthians 10:12

> So, if you think you are standing firm, be careful that you
> don't fall!

Galatians 6:3

> If anyone thinks he is something when he is nothing, he
> deceives himself.

·· Sinful Attitudes: Revenge ····························

Proverbs 19:11

> A man's wisdom gives him patience;
> it is to his glory to overlook an offense.

Proverbs 20:22

> Do not say, "I'll pay you back for this wrong!"
> Wait for the LORD, and he will deliver you.

Proverbs 24:17

> Do not gloat when your enemy falls;
> when he stumbles, do not let your heart rejoice.

Proverbs 24:29

> Do not say, "I'll do to him as he has done to me;
> I'll pay that man back for what he did."

Romans 12:17-19

> Do not repay anyone evil for evil. Be careful to do what is
> right in the eyes of everybody. If it is possible, as far as it
> depends on you, live at peace with everyone. Do not take
> revenge, my friends, but leave room for God's wrath, for it
> is written: "It is mine to avenge; I will repay," says the Lord.

1 Thessalonians 5:15

Make sure that nobody pays back wrong for wrong, but always try to be kind to each other and to everyone else.

1 Peter 3:9

Do not repay evil with evil or insult with insult, but with blessing, because to this you were called so that you may inherit a blessing.

 (Illustration: Matthew 5:38-44—An eye for an eye)

·· Sinful Attitudes: Selfishness ···························

Proverbs 11:24-25

One man gives freely, yet gains even more;
 another withholds unduly, but comes to poverty.
A generous man will prosper;
 he who refreshes others will himself be refreshed.

Proverbs 18:1

An unfriendly man pursues selfish ends;
 he defies all sound judgment.

Isaiah 5:8

Woe to you who add house to house
 and join field to field
till no space is left
 and you live alone in the land.

Philippians 2:3-5

Do nothing out of selfish ambition or vain conceit, but in humility consider others better than yourselves. Each of you should look not only to your own interests, but also to the interests of others. Your attitude should be the same as that of Christ Jesus.

James 3:16

For where you have envy and selfish ambition, there you find disorder and every evil practice.

 (Illustration: Genesis 13—Lot took the better land)

·· Sinful Heart: Troublemaking ······················

Proverbs 6:12-19

A scoundrel and villain,
 who goes about with a corrupt mouth,
 who winks with his eye,

signals with his feet
and motions with his fingers,
who plots evil with deceit in his heart—
he always stirs up dissension.
Therefore disaster will overtake him in an instant;
he will suddenly be destroyed—without remedy.
There are six things the LORD hates,
seven that are detestable to him:
haughty eyes,
a lying tongue,
hands that shed innocent blood,
a heart that devises wicked schemes,
feet that are quick to rush into evil,
a false witness who pours out lies
and a man who stirs up dissension among brothers.

Proverbs 11:29

He who brings trouble on his family will inherit
only wind,
and the fool will be servant to the wise.

Proverbs 14:3

A fool's talk brings a rod to his back,
but the lips of the wise protect them.

Proverbs 16:27

A scoundrel plots evil,
and his speech is like a scorching fire.

Proverbs 20:3

It is to a man's honor to avoid strife,
but every fool is quick to quarrel.

Proverbs 26:4

Do not answer a fool according to his folly,
or you will be like him yourself.

Proverbs 26:21

As charcoal to embers and as wood to fire,
so is a quarrelsome man for kindling strife.

Proverbs 27:22

Though you grind a fool in a mortar,
grinding him like grain with a pestle,
you will not remove his folly from him.

Proverbs 30:32-33

"If you have played the fool and exalted yourself,
   or if you have planned evil,
   clap your hand over your mouth!
For as churning the milk produces butter,
   and as twisting the nose produces blood,
   so stirring up anger produces strife."

(Illustration: Judges 15:3-5—Samson setting fire to foxes' tails)

chapter

Growing in Behavior

··Positive Behavior: Being Prompt and Motivated ········

Proverbs 6:6-8

Go to the ant, you sluggard;
consider its ways and be wise!
It has no commander,
no overseer or ruler,
yet it stores its provisions in summer
and gathers its food at harvest.

Proverbs 20:4

A sluggard does not plow in season;
so at harvest time he looks but finds nothing.

Proverbs 24:33-34

A little sleep, a little slumber,
a little folding of the hands to rest—
and poverty will come on you like a bandit
and scarcity like an armed man.

Ecclesiastes 5:4

When you make a vow to God, do not delay in fulfilling it.
He has no pleasure in fools; fulfill your vow.

Matthew 5:37a

"Simply let your 'Yes' be 'Yes,' and your 'No,' 'No.'"

 (Illustrations: Matthew 25:1-13—Wise and foolish virgins; Luke 12:35-40—Watchful and Ready)

··Positive Behavior: Considering Others ················

1 Corinthians 13:4-5

Love is patient, love is kind. It does not envy, it does not boast, it is not proud. It is not rude, it is not self-seeking, it is not easily angered, it keeps no record of wrongs.

Ephesians 5:21

Submit to one another out of reverence for Christ.

Philippians 2:3-4

Do nothing out of selfish ambition or vain conceit, but in humility consider others better than yourselves. Each of you should look not only to your own interests, but also to the interests of others.

Titus 3:2

[Remind the people] to slander no one, to be peaceable and considerate, and to show true humility toward all men.

James 3:17

But the wisdom that comes from heaven is first of all pure; then peace-loving, considerate, submissive, full of mercy and good fruit, impartial and sincere.

1 Peter 2:17

Show proper respect to everyone: Love the brotherhood of believers, fear God, honor the king.

··Positive Behavior: Following Rules ·····················

1 Corinthians 9:25a

Everyone who competes in the games goes into strict training.

2 Timothy 2:5

Similarly, if anyone competes as an athlete, he does not receive the victor's crown unless he competes according to the rules.

··Positive Behavior: Managing Money ·····················

Proverbs 13:11

Dishonest money dwindles away,
     but he who gathers money little by little
          makes it grow.

Proverbs 16:8

Better a little with righteousness
     than much gain with injustice.

Proverbs 21:6

A fortune made by a lying tongue
     is a fleeting vapor and a deadly snare.

Proverbs 21:17

He who loves pleasure will become poor;
>   whoever loves wine and oil will never be rich.

Proverbs 23:4

Do not wear yourself out to get rich;
>   have the wisdom to show restraint.

Proverbs 28:19-20

He who works his land will have abundant food,
>   but the one who chases fantasies
>   will have his fill of poverty.
A faithful man will be richly blessed,
>   but one eager to get rich will not go unpunished.

Proverbs 30:7-9

"Two things I ask of you, O LORD;
>   do not refuse me before I die:
Keep falsehood and lies far from me;
>   give me neither poverty nor riches,
>   but give me only my daily bread.
Otherwise, I may have too much and disown you
>   and say, 'Who is the LORD?'
Or I may become poor and steal,
>   and so dishonor the name of my God."

1 Thessalonians 4:11-12

Make it your ambition to lead a quiet life, to mind your own business and to work with your hands, just as we told you, so that your daily life may win the respect of outsiders and so that you will not be dependent on anybody.

 (Illustration: Genesis 41:14-36—Joseph managing the kingdom well)

·· Negative Behavior: Accepting/Offering Bribes ··········

Exodus 23:8

"Do not accept a bribe, for a bribe blinds those who see and twists the words of the righteous."

Deuteronomy 27:25

"Cursed is the man who accepts a bribe to kill an
>   innocent person."
>   Then all the people shall say, "Amen!"

Proverbs 6:35
> He will not accept any compensation;
> > he will refuse the bribe, however great it is.

Proverbs 15:27
> A greedy man brings trouble to his family,
> > but he who hates bribes will live.

Proverbs 17:8
> A bribe is a charm to the one who gives it;
> > wherever he turns, he succeeds.

Ecclesiastes 7:7
> Extortion turns a wise man into a fool,
> > and a bribe corrupts the heart.

••Negative Behavior: Cheating ••••••••••••••••••••••

Proverbs 20:10
> Differing weights and differing measures—
> > the LORD detests them both.

Proverbs 20:17
> Food gained by fraud tastes sweet to a man,
> > but he ends up with a mouth full of gravel.

Colossians 3:22-23
> Slaves, obey your earthly masters in everything; and do it, not only when their eye is on you and to win their favor, but with sincerity of heart and reverence for the Lord. Whatever you do, work at it with all your heart, as working for the Lord, not for men.

2 Timothy 2:5
> Similarly, if anyone competes as an athlete, he does not receive the victor's crown unless he competes according to the rules.

 (Illustration: Genesis 27—Jacob cheats Esau)

••Negative Behavior: Loving Money Too Much ••••••••••••

Proverbs 11:4
> Wealth is worthless in the day of wrath,
> > but righteousness delivers from death.

Proverbs 11:28

Whoever trusts in his riches will fall,
but the righteous will thrive like a green leaf.

Proverbs 13:7-8

One man pretends to be rich, yet has nothing;
another pretends to be poor, yet has great wealth.
A man's riches may ransom his life,
but a poor man hears no threat.

Proverbs 15:16-17

Better a little with the fear of the LORD
than great wealth with turmoil.
Better a meal of vegetables where there is love
than a fattened calf with hatred.

Proverbs 22:1-2

A good name is more desirable than great riches;
to be esteemed is better than silver or gold.
Rich and poor have this in common:
The LORD is the Maker of them all.

Proverbs 23:5

Cast but a glance at riches, and they are gone,
for they will surely sprout wings
and fly off to the sky like an eagle.

Ecclesiastes 5:10-14

Whoever loves money never has money enough;
whoever loves wealth is never satisfied
with his income.
This too is meaningless.
As goods increase,
so do those who consume them.
And what benefit are they to the owner
except to feast his eyes on them?
The sleep of a laborer is sweet,
whether he eats little or much,
but the abundance of a rich man
permits him no sleep.
I have seen a grievous evil under the sun:
wealth hoarded to the harm of its owner,
or wealth lost through some misfortune,
so that when he has a son
there is nothing left for him.

Matthew 6:24

"No one can serve two masters. Either he will hate the one and love the other, or he will be devoted to the one and despise the other. You cannot serve both God and Money."

1 Timothy 6:9-10

People who want to get rich fall into temptation and a trap and into many foolish and harmful desires that plunge men into ruin and destruction. For the love of money is a root of all kinds of evil. Some people, eager for money, have wandered from the faith and pierced themselves with many griefs.

Hebrews 13:5

Keep your lives free from the love of money and be content with what you have, because God has said,

"Never will I leave you;
never will I forsake you."

1 John 3:17

If anyone has material possessions and sees his brother in need but has no pity on him, how can the love of God be in him?

 (Illustration: Matthew 19:16-24—Parable of rich young man)

·· Negative Behavior: Procrastinating ····················

Proverbs 27:1

Do not boast about tomorrow,
for you do not know what a day may bring forth.

Luke 9:59-62

He said to another man, "Follow me."

But the man replied, "Lord, first let me go and bury my father."

Jesus said to him, "Let the dead bury their own dead, but you go and proclaim the kingdom of God."

Still another said, "I will follow you, Lord; but first let me go back and say good-by to my family."

Jesus replied, "No one who puts his hand to the plow and looks back is fit for service in the kingdom of God."

Hebrews 3:13

But encourage one another daily, as long as it is called Today, so that none of you may be hardened by sin's deceitfulness.

 (Illustrations: Matthew 25:1-13—Wise and foolish virgins; Acts 24—Felix)

••Negative Behavior: Stealing ••••••••••••••••••••••

Exodus 20:15

"You shall not steal."

Proverbs 1:19

Such is the end of all who go after ill-gotten gain;
    it takes away the lives of those who get it.

Proverbs 10:2

Ill-gotten treasures are of no value,
    but righteousness delivers from death.

Proverbs 16:8

Better a little with righteousness
    than much gain with injustice.

Proverbs 19:26

He who robs his father and drives out his mother
    is a son who brings shame and disgrace.

Proverbs 20:17

Food gained by fraud tastes sweet to a man,
    but he ends up with a mouth full of gravel.

Proverbs 28:24

He who robs his father or mother
    and says, "It's not wrong"—
    he is partner to him who destroys.

Romans 13:9

The commandments... "Do not steal,"...are summed up in this one rule: "Love your neighbor as yourself."

Ephesians 4:28

He who has been stealing must steal no longer, but must work, doing something useful with his own hands, that he may have something to share with those in need.

 (Illustration: Genesis 31—Rachel stealing her father's gods)

chapter

3

Growing in Body

••Alcohol, Drugs and Other Substance Abuse ••••••••••••

Proverbs 20:1

Wine is a mocker and beer a brawler;
whoever is led astray by them is not wise.

Proverbs 21:17

He who loves pleasure will become poor;
whoever loves wine and oil will never be rich.

Proverbs 23:29-35

Who has woe? Who has sorrow?
Who has strife? Who has complaints?
Who has needless bruises? Who has bloodshot eyes?
Those who linger over wine,
who go to sample bowls of mixed wine.
Do not gaze at wine when it is red,
when it sparkles in the cup,
when it goes down smoothly!
In the end it bites like a snake
and poisons like a viper.
Your eyes will see strange sights
and your mind imagine confusing things.
You will be like one sleeping on the high seas,
lying on top of the rigging.
"They hit me," you will say, "but I'm not hurt!
They beat me, but I don't feel it!
When will I wake up
so I can find another drink?"

Isaiah 5:11-12

Woe to those who rise early in the morning
to run after their drinks,
who stay up late at night
till they are inflamed with wine.
They have harps and lyres at their banquets,
tambourines and flutes and wine,
but they have no regard for the deeds of the LORD,
no respect for the work of his hands.

Isaiah 5:22

> Woe to those who are heroes at drinking wine
>   and champions at mixing drinks.

Ephesians 5:18

> Do not get drunk on wine, which leads to debauchery.
> Instead, be filled with the Spirit.

 (Illustration: Genesis 9:18-23—Noah's drunkenness)

··Appearance ·····································

1 Samuel 16:7

> But the LORD said to Samuel, "Do not consider his appear-
> ance or his height, for I have rejected him. The LORD does
> not look at the things man looks at. Man looks at the out-
> ward appearance, but the LORD looks at the heart."

Proverbs 31:30

> Charm is deceptive, and beauty is fleeting;
>   but a woman who fears the LORD is to be praised.

1 Peter 3:3-4

> Your beauty should not come from outward adornment,
> such as braided hair and the wearing of gold jewelry and
> fine clothes. Instead, it should be that of your inner self,
> the unfading beauty of a gentle and quiet spirit, which is
> of great worth in God's sight.

 (Illustration: Esther—An example of inner and outer beauty)

··Body Care ·····································

Romans 6:13

> Do not offer the parts of your body to sin, as instruments
> of wickedness, but rather offer yourselves to God, as those
> who have been brought from death to life; and offer the
> parts of your body to him as instruments of righteousness.

1 Corinthians 3:16-17

> Don't you know that you yourselves are God's temple and
> that God's Spirit lives in you? If anyone destroys God's
> temple, God will destroy him; for God's temple is sacred,
> and you are that temple.

1 Corinthians 6:19-20

> Do you not know that your body is a temple of the Holy
> Spirit, who is in you, whom you have received from God?

You are not your own; you were bought at a price. Therefore honor God with your body.

·· Body Language ··

Proverbs 6:12-18

A scoundrel and villain,
who goes about with a corrupt mouth,
who winks with his eye,
signals with his feet
and motions with his fingers,
who plots evil with deceit in his heart—
he always stirs up dissension.
Therefore disaster will overtake him in an instant;
he will suddenly be destroyed—without remedy.
There are six things the LORD hates,
seven that are detestable to him:
haughty eyes,
a lying tongue,
hands that shed innocent blood,
a heart that devises wicked schemes,
feet that are quick to rush into evil.

Proverbs 10:10a

He who winks maliciously causes grief.

Proverbs 15:30

A cheerful look brings joy to the heart,
and good news gives health to the bones.

Proverbs 16:30

He who winks with his eye is plotting perversity;
he who purses his lips is bent on evil.

Proverbs 21:4

Haughty eyes and a proud heart,
the lamp of the wicked, are sin!

(Illustration: Matthew 26:14-25, 47-50—Judas kissing Jesus)

·· Clothes ···

Matthew 6:28-30

"And why do you worry about clothes? See how the lilies of
the field grow. They do not labor or spin. Yet I tell you that

not even Solomon in all his splendor was dressed like one of these. If that is how God clothes the grass of the field, which is here today and tomorrow is thrown into the fire, will he not much more clothe you, O you of little faith?"

Ephesians 5:3

But among you there must not be even a hint of sexual immorality, or of any kind of impurity, or of greed, because these are improper for God's holy people.

Colossians 3:2

Set your minds on things above, not on earthly things.

1 Timothy 2:9-10

I also want women to dress modestly, with decency and propriety, not with braided hair or gold or pearls or expensive clothes, but with good deeds, appropriate for women who profess to worship God.

··Eating Habits ·····································

Psalm 107:18

They loathed all food
　　and drew near the gates of death.

Proverbs 23:1-3

When you sit to dine with a ruler,
　　note well what is before you,
and put a knife to your throat
　　if you are given to gluttony.
Do not crave his delicacies,
　　for that food is deceptive.

Proverbs 25:16

If you find honey, eat just enough—
　　too much of it, and you will vomit.

Proverbs 25:27

It is not good to eat too much honey,
　　nor is it honorable to seek one's own honor.

Proverbs 27:7

He who is full loathes honey,
　　but to the hungry even what is bitter tastes sweet.

(Illustration: Daniel 1:8-16—Choosing good nutrition)

chapter

4

Growing in Emotions

·· Healthy Emotions: Cheerfulness ·····················

Proverbs 15:13
A happy heart makes the face cheerful,
    but heartache crushes the spirit.

Proverbs 15:15
All the days of the oppressed are wretched,
    but the cheerful heart has a continual feast.

Proverbs 15:30
A cheerful look brings joy to the heart,
    and good news gives health to the bones.

Proverbs 17:22
A cheerful heart is good medicine,
    but a crushed spirit dries up the bones.

·· Healthy Emotions: Joy and Laughter ·················

Psalm 20:4-5
May he give you the desire of your heart
    and make all your plans succeed.
We will shout for joy when you are victorious
    and will lift up our banners in the name of our God.
May the LORD grant all your requests.

Psalm 51:11-12
Do not cast me from your presence
    or take your Holy Spirit from me.
Restore to me the joy of your salvation
    and grant me a willing spirit, to sustain me.

Psalm 94:18-19
When I said, "My foot is slipping,"
    your love, O LORD, supported me.
When anxiety was great within me,
    your consolation brought joy to my soul.

Proverbs 15:30
> A cheerful look brings joy to the heart,
>   and good news gives health to the bones.

Ecclesiastes 11:9
> Be happy, young man, while you are young,
>   and let your heart give you joy in the days
>   of your youth.
> Follow the ways of your heart
>   and whatever your eyes see,
> but know that for all these things
>   God will bring you to judgment.

Luke 10:20
> "However, do not rejoice that the spirits submit to you, but rejoice that your names are written in heaven."

Galatians 5:22-23a
> But the fruit of the Spirit is love, joy, peace, patience, kindness, goodness, faithfulness, gentleness and self-control.

Philippians 4:4
> Rejoice in the Lord always. I will say it again: Rejoice!

1 Thessalonians 5:16
> Be joyful always.

 (Illustration: John 16:17-24—Jesus making joy complete)

·· Healthy Emotions: Self-Control ·····················

Proverbs 4:24-27
> Put away perversity from your mouth;
>   keep corrupt talk far from your lips.
> Let your eyes look straight ahead,
>   fix your gaze directly before you.
> Make level paths for your feet
>   and take only ways that are firm.
> Do not swerve to the right or the left;
>   keep your foot from evil.

Proverbs 25:28
> Like a city whose walls are broken down
>   is a man who lacks self-control.

Proverbs 29:11

A fool gives full vent to his anger,
  but a wise man keeps himself under control.

Galatians 5:22-23

But the fruit of the Spirit is love, joy, peace, patience, kindness, goodness, faithfulness, gentleness and self-control. Against such things there is no law.

1 Thessalonians 5:6-9

So then, let us not be like others, who are asleep, but let us be alert and self-controlled. For those who sleep, sleep at night, and those who get drunk, get drunk at night. But since we belong to the day, let us be self-controlled, putting on faith and love as a breastplate, and the hope of salvation as a helmet. For God did not appoint us to suffer wrath but to receive salvation through our Lord Jesus Christ.

Titus 2:11-12

For the grace of God that brings salvation has appeared to all men. It teaches us to say "No" to ungodliness and worldly passions, and to live self-controlled, upright and godly lives in this present age.

1 Peter 1:13

Therefore, prepare your minds for action; be self-controlled; set your hope fully on the grace to be given you when Jesus Christ is revealed.

1 Peter 5:8

Be self-controlled and alert. Your enemy the devil prowls around like a roaring lion looking for someone to devour.

 (Illustration: Matthew 26:62-63, 27:12-14—Jesus before Pilate)

••Unhealthy Emotions: Anger ••••••••••••••••••••••••

Psalm 4:4

In your anger do not sin;
  when you are on your beds,
  search your hearts and be silent.

Psalm 37:8-9

Refrain from anger and turn from wrath;
  do not fret—it leads only to evil.
For evil men will be cut off,
  but those who hope in the LORD will inherit the land.

Proverbs 15:1

A gentle answer turns away wrath,
but a harsh word stirs up anger.

Proverbs 16:32

Better a patient man than a warrior,
a man who controls his temper than
one who takes a city.

Proverbs 29:11

A fool gives full vent to his anger,
but a wise man keeps himself under control.

Proverbs 29:22

An angry man stirs up dissension,
and a hot-tempered one commits many sins.

Proverbs 30:33

"For as churning the milk produces butter,
and as twisting the nose produces blood,
so stirring up anger produces strife."

Matthew 5:22

"But I tell you that anyone who is angry with his brother
will be subject to judgment. Again, anyone who says to his
brother, 'Raca,' is answerable to the Sanhedrin. But anyone
who says, 'You fool!' will be in danger of the fire of hell."

Ephesians 4:26

"In your anger do not sin": Do not let the sun go down
while you are still angry.

James 1:19-20

My dear brothers, take note of this: Everyone should be
quick to listen, slow to speak and slow to become angry,
for man's anger does not bring about the righteous life
that God desires.

(Illustrations: Genesis 4:3-12—Cain murders Abel; 1 Kings 21:1-6—
Ahab angry with Naboth)

·· Unhealthy Emotions: Fear ·····························

Genesis 26:24a

That night the LORD appeared to him and said, "I am the
God of your father Abraham. Do not be afraid, for I am
with you."

Psalm 27:1

The LORD is my light and my salvation—
  whom shall I fear?
The LORD is the stronghold of my life—
  of whom shall I be afraid?

Proverbs 3:24-26

When you lie down, you will not be afraid;
  when you lie down, your sleep will be sweet.
Have no fear of sudden disaster
  or of the ruin that overtakes the wicked,
for the LORD will be your confidence
  and will keep your foot from being snared.

Isaiah 12:2

"Surely God is my salvation;
  I will trust and not be afraid.
The LORD, the LORD, is my strength and my song;
  he has become my salvation."

Hebrews 13:6

So we say with confidence,

"The Lord is my helper; I will not be afraid.
  What can man do to me?"

··Unhealthy Emotions: Temper ························

Proverbs 14:17

A quick-tempered man does foolish things,
  and a crafty man is hated.

Proverbs 14:29

A patient man has great understanding,
  but a quick-tempered man displays folly.

Proverbs 15:18

A hot-tempered man stirs up dissension,
  but a patient man calms a quarrel.

Proverbs 16:32

Better a patient man than a warrior,
  a man who controls his temper than
    one who takes a city.

Proverbs 17:27

A man of knowledge uses words with restraint,
  and a man of understanding is even-tempered.

Proverbs 19:19

A hot-tempered man must pay the penalty;
    if you rescue him, you will have to do it again.

Proverbs 29:22

An angry man stirs up dissension,
    and a hot-tempered one commits many sins.

·· Unhealthy Emotions: Worry ·······················

Proverbs 3:24–26

When you lie down, you will not be afraid;
    when you lie down, your sleep will be sweet.
Have no fear of sudden disaster
    or of the ruin that overtakes the wicked,
for the LORD will be your confidence
    and will keep your foot from being snared.

Proverbs 12:25

An anxious heart weighs a man down,
    but a kind word cheers him up.

Proverbs 29:25

Fear of man will prove to be a snare,
    but whoever trusts in the LORD is kept safe.

Matthew 6:34

"Therefore do not worry about tomorrow, for tomorrow will worry about itself. Each day has enough trouble of its own."

Matthew 13:22

"The one who received the seed that fell among the thorns is the man who hears the word, but the worries of this life and the deceitfulness of wealth choke it, making it unfruitful."

Philippians 4:4–6

Rejoice in the Lord always. I will say it again: Rejoice! Let your gentleness be evident to all. The Lord is near. Do not be anxious about anything, but in everything, by prayer and petition, with thanksgiving, present your requests to God.

 (Illustration: Matthew 6:25-34—Don't worry about life)

chapter 5

Growing in Mind

••Accepting Advice •••••••••••••••••••••••••••••••

Proverbs 11:14
> For lack of guidance a nation falls,
> but many advisers make victory sure.

Proverbs 13:10
> Pride only breeds quarrels,
> but wisdom is found in those who take advice.

Proverbs 15:12
> A mocker resents correction;
> he will not consult the wise.

Proverbs 15:22
> Plans fail for lack of counsel,
> but with many advisers they succeed.

Proverbs 20:18
> Make plans by seeking advice;
> if you wage war, obtain guidance.

Proverbs 24:5-6
> A wise man has great power,
> and a man of knowledge increases strength;
> for waging war you need guidance,
> and for victory many advisers.

 (Illustration: Esther 2:10-16—Esther seeks advice)

••Daydreaming ••••••••••••••••••••••••••••••••••

Proverbs 12:11
> He who works his land will have abundant food,
> but he who chases fantasies lacks judgment.

Proverbs 28:19
> He who works his land will have abundant food,
> but the one who chases fantasies will
> have his fill of poverty.

Ecclesiastes 5:7
Much dreaming and many words are meaningless.
Therefore stand in awe of God.

Isaiah 56:10b
...they lie around and dream,
they love to sleep.

•• Finding Wisdom •••••••••••••••••••••••••••••••••

Psalm 111:10a
The fear of the LORD is the beginning of wisdom.

Proverbs 1:7
The fear of the LORD is the beginning of knowledge,
but fools despise wisdom and discipline.

Proverbs 2:6
For the LORD gives wisdom,
and from his mouth come knowledge
and understanding.

Proverbs 2:12-15
Wisdom will save you from the ways of wicked men,
from men whose words are perverse,
who leave the straight paths
to walk in dark ways,
who delight in doing wrong
and rejoice in the perverseness of evil,
whose paths are crooked
and who are devious in their ways.

Proverbs 8:10-11
"Choose my instruction instead of silver,
knowledge rather than choice gold,
for wisdom is more precious than rubies,
and nothing you desire can compare with her."

Proverbs 16:16
How much better to get wisdom than gold,
to choose understanding rather than silver!

1 Corinthians 3:18-19
Do not deceive yourselves. If any one of you thinks he is
wise by the standards of this age, he should become a
"fool" so that he may become wise. For the wisdom of this

world is foolishness in God's sight. As it is written: "He catches the wise in their craftiness."

 (Illustration: 1 Kings 3:7-15; 4:29-34—Solomon asks God for wisdom)

·· Making Decisions ·····································

Proverbs 3:7-8

Do not be wise in your own eyes;
    fear the LORD and shun evil.
This will bring health to your body
    and nourishment to your bones.

Proverbs 12:15

The way of a fool seems right to him,
    but a wise man listens to advice.

Proverbs 14:12

There is a way that seems right to a man,
    but in the end it leads to death.

Proverbs 14:15-16

A simple man believes anything,
    but a prudent man gives thought to his steps.
A wise man fears the LORD and shuns evil,
    but a fool is hotheaded and reckless.

Proverbs 18:17

The first to present his case seems right,
    till another comes forward and questions him.

Proverbs 19:2

It is not good to have zeal without knowledge,
    nor to be hasty and miss the way.

Proverbs 21:29

A wicked man puts up a bold front,
    but an upright man gives thought to his ways.

Proverbs 22:3

A prudent man sees danger and takes refuge,
    but the simple keep going and suffer for it.

Ephesians 5:15

Be very careful, then, how you live—not as unwise
but as wise.

Colossians 2:8

See to it that no one takes you captive through hollow and deceptive philosophy, which depends on human tradition and the basic principles of this world rather than on Christ.

·· Planning Carefully ·······································

Proverbs 14:22

Do not those who plot evil go astray?
But those who plan what is good find love
and faithfulness.

Proverbs 15:22

Plans fail for lack of counsel,
but with many advisers they succeed.

Proverbs 16:3

Commit to the LORD whatever you do,
and your plans will succeed.

Proverbs 19:21

Many are the plans in a man's heart,
but it is the LORD's purpose that prevails.

Proverbs 21:30

There is no wisdom, no insight, no plan
that can succeed against the LORD.

James 4:13-15

Now listen, you who say, "Today or tomorrow we will go to this or that city, spend a year there, carry on business and make money." Why, you do not even know what will happen tomorrow. What is your life? You are a mist that appears for a little while and then vanishes. Instead, you ought to say, "If it is the Lord's will, we will live and do this or that."

·· Receiving Instruction ·······························

Proverbs 1:8-9

Listen, my son, to your father's instruction
and do not forsake your mother's teaching.
They will be a garland to grace your head
and a chain to adorn your neck.

Proverbs 4:10-14

> Listen, my son, accept what I say,
> > and the years of your life will be many.
> I guide you in the way of wisdom
> > and lead you along straight paths.
> When you walk, your steps will not be hampered;
> > when you run, you will not stumble.
> Hold on to instruction, do not let it go;
> > guard it well, for it is your life.
> Do not set foot on the path of the wicked
> > or walk in the way of evil men.

Proverbs 8:10

> "Choose my instruction instead of silver,
> > knowledge rather than choice gold."

Proverbs 13:1

> A wise son heeds his father's instruction,
> > but a mocker does not listen to rebuke.

1 Thessalonians 4:7-8

> For God did not call us to be impure, but to live a holy life. Therefore, he who rejects this instruction does not reject man but God, who gives you his Holy Spirit.

 (Illustration: Ruth 3:1-6—Ruth obeys her mother-in-law)

··Resisting Temptation ·································

Proverbs 1:10-15

> My son, if sinners entice you,
> > do not give in to them.
> If they say, "Come along with us;
> > let's lie in wait for someone's blood,
> > let's waylay some harmless soul;
> let's swallow them alive, like the grave,
> > and whole, like those who go down to the pit;
> we will get all sorts of valuable things
> > and fill our houses with plunder;
> throw in your lot with us,
> > and we will share a common purse"—
> my son, do not go along with them,
> > do not set foot on their paths.

Proverbs 4:14-15

Do not set foot on the path of the wicked
  or walk in the way of evil men.
Avoid it, do not travel on it;
  turn from it and go on your way.

Isaiah 33:15-16a

He who walks righteously
  and speaks what is right,
who rejects gain from extortion
  and keeps his hand from accepting bribes,
who stops his ears against plots of murder
  and shuts his eyes against contemplating evil—
this is the man who will dwell on the heights,
  whose refuge will be the mountain fortress.

Hebrews 2:18

Because he himself suffered when he was tempted, he is
able to help those who are being tempted.

Hebrews 4:15

For we do not have a high priest who is unable to sympa-
thize with our weaknesses, but we have one who has been
tempted in every way, just as we are—yet was without sin.

James 1:13-15

When tempted, no one should say, "God is tempting me."
For God cannot be tempted by evil, nor does he tempt
anyone; but each one is tempted when, by his own evil
desire, he is dragged away and enticed. Then, after desire
has conceived, it gives birth to sin; and sin, when it is full-
grown, gives birth to death.

James 4:7

Submit yourselves, then, to God. Resist the devil, and he
will flee from you.

 (Illustration: Matthew 4:1-4—Jesus resists temptation)

·· Thinking Good Thoughts ····························

Proverbs 15:26

The LORD detests the thoughts of the wicked,
  but those of the pure are pleasing to him.

Romans 8:6

The mind of sinful man is death, but the mind controlled by the Spirit is life and peace.

Philippians 4:8

Finally, brothers, whatever is true, whatever is noble, whatever is right, whatever is pure, whatever is lovely, whatever is admirable—if anything is excellent or praiseworthy—think about such things.

Colossians 3:2

Set your minds on things above, not on earthly things.

chapter

6

Growing in Relationships

•• The Pluses: Fairness ••••••••••••••••••••••••••••••••••

Proverbs 17:15
Acquitting the guilty and condemning the innocent—
the LORD detests them both.

Proverbs 24:23-25
These also are sayings of the wise:
To show partiality in judging is not good:
Whoever says to the guilty, "You are innocent"—
peoples will curse him and nations denounce him.
But it will go well with those who convict the guilty,
and rich blessing will come upon them.

Matthew 7:2
"For in the same way you judge others, you will be judged,
and with the measure you use, it will be measured to you."

Matthew 16:27
"For the Son of Man is going to come in his Father's glory
with his angels, and then he will reward each person
according to what he has done."

Galatians 6:7
Do not be deceived: God cannot be mocked. A man reaps
what he sows.

•• The Pluses: Friendships ••••••••••••••••••••••••••••••

Proverbs 12:26
A righteous man is cautious in friendship,
but the way of the wicked leads them astray.

Proverbs 17:17
A friend loves at all times,
and a brother is born for adversity.

Proverbs 18:24
A man of many companions may come to ruin,
but there is a friend who sticks closer than a brother.

Proverbs 27:9

Perfume and incense bring joy to the heart,
> and the pleasantness of one's friend springs from his
> earnest counsel.

Ecclesiastes 4:9-11

Two are better than one,
> because they have a good return for their work:
If one falls down,
> his friend can help him up.
But pity the man who falls
> and has no one to help him up!
Also, if two lie down together, they will keep warm.
> But how can one keep warm alone?

John 15:13-15

"Greater love has no one than this, that he lay down his
life for his friends. You are my friends if you do what I command. I no longer call you servants, because a servant
does not know his master's business. Instead, I have called
you friends, for everything that I learned from my Father I
have made known to you."

(Illustrations: Ruth 1:1-19—Ruth and Naomi; 1 Samuel 20—Jonathan
and David)

·· The Pluses: Peacemaking ·······························

Proverbs 12:20

There is deceit in the hearts of those who plot evil,
> but joy for those who promote peace.

Proverbs 15:1

A gentle answer turns away wrath,
> but a harsh word stirs up anger.

Proverbs 16:7

When a man's ways are pleasing to the LORD,
> he makes even his enemies live at peace with him.

Proverbs 17:1

Better a dry crust with peace and quiet
> than a house full of feasting, with strife.

Proverbs 17:14

Starting a quarrel is like breaching a dam;
> so drop the matter before a dispute breaks out.

Proverbs 18:18

Casting the lot settles disputes
and keeps strong opponents apart.

Matthew 5:9

"Blessed are the peacemakers,
for they will be called sons of God."

Matthew 5:39-40

"But I tell you, Do not resist an evil person. If someone strikes you on the right cheek, turn to him the other also. And if someone wants to sue you and take your tunic, let him have your cloak as well."

Romans 12:18

If it is possible, as far as it depends on you, live at peace with everyone.

Romans 14:19

Let us therefore make every effort to do what leads to peace and to mutual edification.

2 Timothy 2:23

Don't have anything to do with foolish and stupid arguments, because you know they produce quarrels.

James 3:18

Peacemakers who sow in peace raise a harvest of righteousness.

•• The Pluses: Standing Up for Your Beliefs ••••••••••••••

1 Samuel 8:7

And the LORD told him: "Listen to all that the people are saying to you; it is not you they have rejected, but they have rejected me as their king."

Matthew 10:22

"All men will hate you because of me, but he who stands firm to the end will be saved."

John 15:18-21

"If the world hates you, keep in mind that it hated me first. If you belonged to the world, it would love you as its own. As it is, you do not belong to the world, but I have chosen you out of the world. That is why the world hates you.

Remember the words I spoke to you: 'No servant is greater than his master.' If they persecuted me, they will persecute you also. If they obeyed my teaching, they will obey yours also. They will treat you this way because of my name, for they do not know the One who sent me."

Acts 4:19-20

But Peter and John replied, "Judge for yourselves whether it is right in God's sight to obey you rather than God. For we cannot help speaking about what we have seen and heard."

2 Corinthians 12:10

That is why, for Christ's sake, I delight in weaknesses, in insults, in hardships, in persecutions, in difficulties. For when I am weak, then I am strong.

1 Peter 2:23

When they hurled their insults at him, he did not retaliate; when he suffered, he made no threats. Instead, he entrusted himself to him who judges justly.

1 Peter 4:12-16

Dear friends, do not be surprised at the painful trial you are suffering, as though something strange were happening to you. But rejoice that you participate in the sufferings of Christ, so that you may be overjoyed when his glory is revealed. If you are insulted because of the name of Christ, you are blessed, for the Spirit of glory and of God rests on you. If you suffer, it should not be as a murderer or thief or any other kind of criminal, or even as a meddler. However, if you suffer as a Christian, do not be ashamed, but praise God that you bear that name.

•• The Minuses: Favoritism ••••••••••••••••••••••••••••••

Leviticus 19:15

"Do not pervert justice; do not show partiality to the poor or favoritism to the great, but judge your neighbor fairly."

Proverbs 18:5

It is not good to be partial to the wicked
or to deprive the innocent of justice.

Proverbs 28:21

To show partiality is not good—
yet a man will do wrong for a piece of bread.

Romans 2:11

For God does not show favoritism.

1 Timothy 5:21

I charge you, in the sight of God and Christ Jesus and the elect angels, to keep these instructions without partiality, and to do nothing out of favoritism.

James 3:17

But the wisdom that comes from heaven is first of all pure; then peace-loving, considerate, submissive, full of mercy and good fruit, impartial and sincere.

•• The Minuses: Judging Others ••••••••••••••••••••••••

1 Samuel 16:7b

"Man looks at the outward appearance, but the LORD looks at the heart."

Matthew 7:1-5

"Do not judge, or you too will be judged. For in the same way you judge others, you will be judged, and with the measure you use, it will be measured to you.

"Why do you look at the speck of sawdust in your brother's eye and pay no attention to the plank in your own eye? How can you say to your brother, 'Let me take the speck out of your eye,' when all the time there is a plank in your own eye? You hypocrite, first take the plank out of your own eye, and then you will see clearly to remove the speck from your brother's eye."

John 7:24

"Stop judging by mere appearances, and make a right judgment."

Romans 2:1-4

You, therefore, have no excuse, you who pass judgment on someone else, for at whatever point you judge the other, you are condemning yourself, because you who pass judgment do the same things. Now we know that God's judgment against those who do such things is based on truth. So when you, a mere man, pass judgment on them and yet do the same things, do you think you will escape God's judgment? Or do you show contempt for the riches of his kindness, tolerance and patience, not realizing that God's kindness leads you toward repentance?

James 4:11-12

Brothers, do not slander one another. Anyone who speaks against his brother or judges him speaks against the law and judges it. When you judge the law, you are not keeping it, but sitting in judgment on it. There is only one Lawgiver and Judge, the one who is able to save and destroy. But you—who are you to judge your neighbor?

•• The Minuses: Peer Pressure ••••••••••••••••••••••••••••

Exodus 23:2a

"Do not follow the crowd in doing wrong."

Psalm 1:1

Blessed is the man
   who does not walk in the counsel of the wicked
or stand in the way of sinners
   or sit in the seat of mockers.

Proverbs 3:31

Do not envy a violent man
   or choose any of his ways.

Proverbs 4:14-17

Do not set foot on the path of the wicked
   or walk in the way of evil men.
Avoid it, do not travel on it;
   turn from it and go on your way.
For they cannot sleep till they do evil;
   they are robbed of slumber till they make
      someone fall.
They eat the bread of wickedness
   and drink the wine of violence.

Proverbs 12:26

A righteous man is cautious in friendship,
   but the way of the wicked leads them astray.

Proverbs 13:20

He who walks with the wise grows wise,
   but a companion of fools suffers harm.

Proverbs 14:7

Stay away from a foolish man,
   for you will not find knowledge on his lips.

Proverbs 14:12

There is a way that seems right to a man,
   but in the end it leads to death.

Proverbs 22:24-25

Do not make friends with a hot-tempered man,
   do not associate with one easily angered,
or you may learn his ways
   and get yourself ensnared.

Proverbs 23:20-21

Do not join those who drink too much wine
   or gorge themselves on meat,
for drunkards and gluttons become poor,
   and drowsiness clothes them in rags.

Proverbs 24:19-20

Do not fret because of evil men
   or be envious of the wicked,
for the evil man has no future hope,
   and the lamp of the wicked will be snuffed out.

Acts 5:29

Peter and the other apostles replied: "We must obey God rather than men!"

Romans 12:2

Do not conform any longer to the pattern of this world, but be transformed by the renewing of your mind. Then you will be able to test and approve what God's will is—his good, pleasing and perfect will.

Romans 16:17-18

I urge you, brothers, to watch out for those who cause divisions and put obstacles in your way that are contrary to the teaching you have learned. Keep away from them. For such people are not serving our Lord Christ, but their own appetites. By smooth talk and flattery they deceive the minds of naive people.

1 Corinthians 5:9

I have written you in my letter not to associate with sexually immoral people.

1 Corinthians 15:33

Do not be misled: "Bad company corrupts good character."

2 Corinthians 6:14

Do not be yoked together with unbelievers. For what do righteousness and wickedness have in common? Or what fellowship can light have with darkness?

2 Timothy 3:12

In fact, everyone who wants to live a godly life in Christ Jesus will be persecuted.

James 4:4

You adulterous people, don't you know that friendship with the world is hatred toward God? Anyone who chooses to be a friend of the world becomes an enemy of God.

2 Peter 3:17-18

Therefore, dear friends, since you already know this, be on your guard so that you may not be carried away by the error of lawless men and fall from your secure position. But grow in the grace and knowledge of our Lord and Savior Jesus Christ. To him be glory both now and forever! Amen.

•• The Minuses: Quarreling ••••••••••••••••••••••••••

Proverbs 15:18

A hot-tempered man stirs up dissension,
but a patient man calms a quarrel.

Proverbs 17:19

He who loves a quarrel loves sin;
he who builds a high gate invites destruction.

Proverbs 20:3

It is to a man's honor to avoid strife,
but every fool is quick to quarrel.

Proverbs 24:28-29

Do not testify against your neighbor without cause,
or use your lips to deceive.
Do not say, "I'll do to him as he has done to me;
I'll pay that man back for what he did."

Proverbs 26:20-21

Without wood a fire goes out;
without gossip a quarrel dies down.
As charcoal to embers and as wood to fire,
so is a quarrelsome man for kindling strife.

Proverbs 28:25

A greedy man stirs up dissension,
> but he who trusts in the LORD will prosper.

Matthew 5:25

"Settle matters quickly with your adversary who is taking you to court. Do it while you are still with him on the way, or he may hand you over to the judge, and the judge may hand you over to the officer, and you may be thrown into prison."

1 Corinthians 3:3

You are still worldly. For since there is jealousy and quarreling among you, are you not worldly? Are you not acting like mere men?

James 4:1-2

What causes fights and quarrels among you? Don't they come from your desires that battle within you? You want something but don't get it. You kill and covet, but you cannot have what you want. You quarrel and fight. You do not have, because you do not ask God.

 (Illustration: Matthew 18:15-17—How to handle disagreement)

chapter

7

Growing in Responsibility

•• Parent's Responsibility: Disciplining ••••••••••••••••••

Proverbs 13:24
> He who spares the rod hates his son,
>> but he who loves him is careful to discipline him.

Proverbs 19:18
> Discipline your son, for in that there is hope;
>> do not be a willing party to his death.

Proverbs 22:15
> Folly is bound up in the heart of a child,
>> but the rod of discipline will drive it far from him.

Proverbs 23:13-14
> Do not withhold discipline from a child;
>> if you punish him with the rod, he will not die.
>
> Punish him with the rod
>> and save his soul from death.

Proverbs 29:15
> The rod of correction imparts wisdom,
>> but a child left to himself disgraces his mother.

Proverbs 29:17
> Discipline your son, and he will give you peace;
>> he will bring delight to your soul.

Ecclesiastes 8:11
> When the sentence for a crime is not quickly carried out, the hearts of the people are filled with schemes to do wrong.

Colossians 3:21
> Fathers, do not embitter your children, or they will become discouraged.

··Parent's Responsibility: Instructing ···················

Deuteronomy 6:6-9

These commandments that I give you today are to be upon your hearts. Impress them on your children. Talk about them when you sit at home and when you walk along the road, when you lie down and when you get up. Tie them as symbols on your hands and bind them on your foreheads. Write them on the doorframes of your houses and on your gates.

Deuteronomy 11:18-19

Fix these words of mine in your hearts and minds; tie them as symbols on your hands and bind them on your foreheads. Teach them to your children, talking about them when you sit at home and when you walk along the road, when you lie down and when you get up.

Psalm 78:1-6

O my people, hear my teaching;
    listen to the words of my mouth.
I will open my mouth in parables,
    I will utter hidden things, things from of old—
what we have heard and known,
    what our fathers have told us.
We will not hide them from their children;
    we will tell the next generation
the praiseworthy deeds of the LORD,
    his power, and the wonders he has done.
He decreed statutes for Jacob
    and established the law in Israel,
which he commanded our forefathers
    to teach their children,
so the next generation would know them,
    even the children yet to be born,
    and they in turn would tell their children.

Proverbs 22:6

Train a child in the way he should go,
    and when he is old he will not turn from it.

Joel 1:3

Tell it to your children,
and let your children tell it to their children,
and their children to the next generation.

Ephesians 6:4

Fathers, do not exasperate your children; instead, bring
them up in the training and instruction of the Lord.

•• Parent's Responsibility: Preventing Abuse ••••••••••••••

Ephesians 4:29

Do not let any unwholesome talk come out of your mouths,
but only what is helpful for building others up according to
their needs, that it may benefit those who listen.

Ephesians 4:31-32

Get rid of all bitterness, rage and anger, brawling and slander, along with every form of malice. Be kind and compassionate to one another, forgiving each other, just as in
Christ God forgave you.

Ephesians 5:3

But among you there must not be even a hint of sexual
immorality, or of any kind of impurity, or of greed, because these are improper for God's holy people.

Ephesians 6:4

Fathers, do not exasperate your children; instead, bring
them up in the training and instruction of the Lord.

Colossians 3:21

Fathers, do not embitter your children, or they will become
discouraged.

1 John 4:18

There is no fear in love. But perfect love drives out fear,
because fear has to do with punishment. The one who
fears is not made perfect in love.

•• Parent's Responsibility: Providing Security ••••••••••••••

Matthew 2:13-14

When they had gone, an angel of the Lord appeared to
Joseph in a dream. "Get up," he said, "take the child and
his mother and escape to Egypt. Stay there until I tell you,
for Herod is going to search for the child to kill him."

So he got up, took the child and his mother during the night and left for Egypt.

1 Timothy 5:8

If anyone does not provide for his relatives, and especially for his immediate family, he has denied the faith and is worse than an unbeliever.

 (Illustration: Hebrews 11:23—Moses hidden by his parents)

••Children's Responsibility: Accepting Proper Discipline ••••

Job 5:17

"Blessed is the man whom God corrects;
so do not despise the discipline of the Almighty."

Proverbs 1:7

The fear of the LORD is the beginning of knowledge,
but fools despise wisdom and discipline.

Proverbs 10:17

He who heeds discipline shows the way to life,
but whoever ignores correction leads others astray.

Proverbs 12:1

Whoever loves discipline loves knowledge,
but he who hates correction is stupid.

Proverbs 13:18

He who ignores discipline comes to poverty and shame,
but whoever heeds correction is honored.

Proverbs 14:9

Fools mock at making amends for sin,
but goodwill is found among the upright.

Proverbs 15:5

A fool spurns his father's discipline,
but whoever heeds correction shows prudence.

Proverbs 15:31-32

He who listens to a life-giving rebuke
will be at home among the wise.
He who ignores discipline despises himself,
but whoever heeds correction gains understanding.

Proverbs 17:10

A rebuke impresses a man of discernment
more than a hundred lashes a fool.

Hebrews 12:8

If you are not disciplined (and everyone undergoes discipline), then you are illegitimate children and not true sons.

·· Children's Responsibility: Listening ····················

Proverbs 1:8-9

Listen, my son, to your father's instruction
    and do not forsake your mother's teaching.
They will be a garland to grace your head
    and a chain to adorn your neck.

Proverbs 3:1-4

My son, do not forget my teaching,
    but keep my commands in your heart,
for they will prolong your life many years
    and bring you prosperity.
Let love and faithfulness never leave you;
    bind them around your neck,
    write them on the tablet of your heart.
Then you will win favor and a good name
    in the sight of God and man.

Proverbs 4:1-4

Listen, my sons, to a father's instruction;
    pay attention and gain understanding.
I give you sound learning,
    so do not forsake my teaching.
When I was a boy in my father's house,
    still tender, and an only child of my mother,
he taught me and said,
    "Lay hold of my words with all your heart;
    keep my commands and you will live."

Proverbs 4:10-13

Listen, my son, accept what I say,
    and the years of your life will be many.
I guide you in the way of wisdom
    and lead you along straight paths.
When you walk, your steps will not be hampered;
    when you run, you will not stumble.
Hold on to instruction, do not let it go;
    guard it well, for it is your life.

Proverbs 5:1-2

> My son, pay attention to my wisdom,
>> listen well to my words of insight,
> that you may maintain discretion
>> and your lips may preserve knowledge.

Proverbs 5:11-14

> At the end of your life you will groan,
>> when your flesh and body are spent.
> You will say, "How I hated discipline!
>> How my heart spurned correction!
> I would not obey my teachers
>> or listen to my instructors.
> I have come to the brink of utter ruin
>> in the midst of the whole assembly."

Proverbs 19:20

> Listen to advice and accept instruction,
>> and in the end you will be wise.

Proverbs 23:22

> Listen to your father, who gave you life,
>> and do not despise your mother when she is old.

··Children's Responsibility: Obeying ····················

Proverbs 6:20-22

> My son, keep your father's commands
>> and do not forsake your mother's teaching.
> Bind them upon your heart forever;
>> fasten them around your neck.
> When you walk, they will guide you;
>> when you sleep, they will watch over you;
>> when you awake, they will speak to you.

Proverbs 13:1

> A wise son heeds his father's instruction,
>> but a mocker does not listen to rebuke.

Proverbs 19:16

> He who obeys instructions guards his life,
>> but he who is contemptuous of his ways will die.

Proverbs 30:17

> "The eye that mocks a father,
>> that scorns obedience to a mother,

will be pecked out by the ravens of the valley,
    will be eaten by the vultures."

Ephesians 6:1

Children, obey your parents in the Lord, for this is right.

Colossians 3:20

Children, obey your parents in everything, for this pleases
the Lord.

··Children's Responsibility: Respecting Authority ··········

Exodus 20:12

"Honor your father and your mother, so that you may live
long in the land the LORD your God is giving you."

Leviticus 19:3

"Each of you must respect his mother and father, and you
must observe my Sabbaths. I am the LORD your God."

Proverbs 13:13

He who scorns instruction will pay for it,
    but he who respects a command is rewarded.

Romans 13:1-2

Everyone must submit himself to the governing authorities, for there is no authority except that which God has
established. The authorities that exist have been established by God. Consequently, he who rebels against the
authority is rebelling against what God has instituted, and
those who do so will bring judgment on themselves.

Titus 3:1-2

Remind the people to be subject to rulers and authorities,
to be obedient, to be ready to do whatever is good, to
slander no one, to be peaceable and considerate, and to
show true humility toward all men.

Hebrews 13:17

Obey your leaders and submit to their authority. They keep
watch over you as men who must give an account. Obey
them so that their work will be a joy, not a burden, for that
would be of no advantage to you.

1 Peter 2:13a

Submit yourselves for the Lord's sake to every authority
instituted among men.

·· Everyone's Responsibility: Accountability ··············

Ecclesiastes 12:14

For God will bring every deed into judgment,
including every hidden thing,
whether it is good or evil.

Matthew 12:36-37

"But I tell you that men will have to give account on the
day of judgment for every careless word they have spoken.
For by your words you will be acquitted, and by your
words you will be condemned."

Romans 14:12

So then, each of us will give an account of himself to God.

Galatians 6:4-5

Each one should test his own actions. Then he can take
pride in himself, without comparing himself to somebody
else, for each one should carry his own load.

Colossians 3:23-25

Whatever you do, work at it with all your heart, as working for the Lord, not for men, since you know that you will
receive an inheritance from the Lord as a reward. It is the
Lord Christ you are serving. Anyone who does wrong will
be repaid for his wrong, and there is no favoritism.

chapter **8**

Growing in Self-Concept

Acceptance
Confidence
Courage
Humility
Reputation

··Acceptance ·····································

Psalm 127:3-5

Sons are a heritage from the LORD,
    children a reward from him.
Like arrows in the hands of a warrior
    are sons born in one's youth.
Blessed is the man
    whose quiver is full of them.
They will not be put to shame
    when they contend with their enemies in the gate.

Mark 10:13-15

People were bringing little children to Jesus to have him
touch them, but the disciples rebuked them. When Jesus
saw this, he was indignant. He said to them, "Let the little
children come to me, and do not hinder them, for the
kingdom of God belongs to such as these. I tell you the
truth, anyone who will not receive the kingdom of God
like a little child will never enter it."

Romans 15:7

Accept one another, then, just as Christ accepted you, in
order to bring praise to God.

1 John 4:10a

This is love: not that we loved God, but that he loved us.

1 John 4:19

We love because he first loved us.

··Confidence ·····································

Proverbs 3:26

For the LORD will be your confidence
    and will keep your foot from being snared.

2 Corinthians 3:5

Not that we are competent in ourselves to claim anything
for ourselves, but our competence comes from God.

Ephesians 3:12

In him and through faith in him we may approach God with freedom and confidence.

Ephesians 3:20

Now to him who is able to do immeasurably more than all we ask or imagine, according to his power that is at work within us...

Philippians 4:13

I can do everything through him who gives me strength.

1 Timothy 4:12

Don't let anyone look down on you because you are young, but set an example for the believers in speech, in life, in love, in faith and in purity.

 (Illustration: 1 Samuel 1—Samuel and his mother Hannah)

·· Courage ··

2 Samuel 2:7a

"Now then, be strong and brave..."

Proverbs 28:1

The wicked man flees though no one pursues,
    but the righteous are as bold as a lion.

Luke 9:26

"If anyone is ashamed of me and my words, the Son of Man will be ashamed of him when he comes in his glory and in the glory of the Father and of the holy angels."

Romans 1:16

I am not ashamed of the gospel, because it is the power of God for the salvation of everyone who believes: first for the Jew, then for the Gentile.

2 Timothy 1:8

So do not be ashamed to testify about our Lord, or ashamed of me his prisoner. But join with me in suffering for the gospel, by the power of God.

2 Timothy 2:15

Do your best to present yourself to God as one approved, a workman who does not need to be ashamed and who correctly handles the word of truth.

Hebrews 13:6

So we say with confidence,

> "The Lord is my helper; I will not be afraid.
>   What can man do to me?"

 (Illustrations: Esther 4:15-16—Esther going before the king; Daniel 3:16-18—Shadrach, Meshach and Abednego)

·· Humility ·······································

Proverbs 16:19

Better to be lowly in spirit and among the oppressed
    than to share plunder with the proud.

Proverbs 22:4

Humility and the fear of the LORD
    bring wealth and honor and life.

Proverbs 25:6-7

Do not exalt yourself in the king's presence,
    and do not claim a place among great men;
it is better for him to say to you, "Come up here,"
    than for him to humiliate you before a nobleman.

Proverbs 27:2

Let another praise you, and not your own mouth;
    someone else, and not your own lips.

Philippians 2:3

Do nothing out of selfish ambition or vain conceit, but in humility consider others better than yourselves.

James 4:10

Humble yourselves before the Lord, and he will lift you up.

1 Peter 5:5-6

Young men, in the same way be submissive to those who are older. All of you, clothe yourselves with humility toward one another, because,

> "God opposes the proud
>   but gives grace to the humble."

Humble yourselves, therefore, under God's mighty hand, that he may lift you up in due time.

 (Illustration: Luke 14:8-11—Positions at the wedding feast)

··Reputation ·······································

Proverbs 20:11
Even a child is known by his actions,
    by whether his conduct is pure and right.

Proverbs 22:1
A good name is more desirable than great riches;
    to be esteemed is better than silver or gold.

1 Timothy 5:24-25
The sins of some men are obvious, reaching the place of
judgment ahead of them; the sins of others trail behind
them. In the same way, good deeds are obvious, and even
those that are not cannot be hidden.

chapter 9

Growing in Sexual Maturity

·· Sexual Warnings: Homosexuality and Incest ··············

Romans 1:26-27

Because of this, God gave them over to shameful lusts. Even their women exchanged natural relations for unnatural ones. In the same way the men also abandoned natural relations with women and were inflamed with lust for one another. Men committed indecent acts with other men, and received in themselves the due penalty for their perversion.

1 Corinthians 5:1

It is actually reported that there is sexual immorality among you, and of a kind that does not occur even among pagans: A man has his father's wife.

1 Corinthians 6:9-10

Do you not know that the wicked will not inherit the kingdom of God? Do not be deceived: Neither the sexually immoral nor idolaters nor adulterers nor male prostitutes nor homosexual offenders nor thieves nor the greedy nor drunkards nor slanderers nor swindlers will inherit the kingdom of God.

 (Illustration: Genesis 19—The men of Sodom and Lot's daughters)

·· Sexual Warnings: Immorality ·························

Ecclesiastes 7:26

I find more bitter than death
  the woman who is a snare,
whose heart is a trap
  and whose hands are chains.
The man who pleases God will escape her,
  but the sinner she will ensnare.

Romans 1:24

Therefore God gave them over in the sinful desires of their hearts to sexual impurity for the degrading of their bodies with one another.

90

Romans 6:12–13

Therefore do not let sin reign in your mortal body so that you obey its evil desires. Do not offer the parts of your body to sin, as instruments of wickedness, but rather offer yourselves to God, as those who have been brought from death to life; and offer the parts of your body to him as instruments of righteousness.

1 Corinthians 5:9

I have written you in my letter not to associate with sexually immoral people.

1 Corinthians 6:13

"Food for the stomach and the stomach for food"—but God will destroy them both. The body is not meant for sexual immorality, but for the Lord, and the Lord for the body.

1 Corinthians 6:18

Flee from sexual immorality. All other sins a man commits are outside his body, but he who sins sexually sins against his own body.

Ephesians 5:5

For of this you can be sure: No immoral, impure or greedy person—such a man is an idolater—has any inheritance in the kingdom of Christ and of God.

Colossians 3:5–6

Put to death, therefore, whatever belongs to your earthly nature: sexual immorality, impurity, lust, evil desires and greed, which is idolatry. Because of these, the wrath of God is coming.

 (Illustration: Proverbs 5, 6, 7—Description of immorality)

••Sexual Warnings: Prostitution ••••••••••••••••••••••••

Proverbs 23:26–28

My son, give me your heart
   and let your eyes keep to my ways,
for a prostitute is a deep pit
   and a wayward wife is a narrow well.
Like a bandit she lies in wait,
   and multiplies the unfaithful among men.

Proverbs 29:3

A man who loves wisdom brings joy to his father,
but a companion of prostitutes squanders his wealth.

1 Corinthians 6:15-16

Do you not know that your bodies are members of Christ himself? Shall I then take the members of Christ and unite them with a prostitute? Never! Do you not know that he who unites himself with a prostitute is one with her in body? For it is said, "The two will become one flesh."

•• Marriage: Preparation (Dating) ••••••••••••••••••••

1 Corinthians 15:33

Do not be misled: "Bad company corrupts good character."

2 Corinthians 6:14-16

Do not be yoked together with unbelievers. For what do righteousness and wickedness have in common? Or what fellowship can light have with darkness? What harmony is there between Christ and Belial? What does a believer have in common with an unbeliever? What agreement is there between the temple of God and idols? For we are the temple of the living God. As God has said: "I will live with them and walk among them, and I will be their God, and they will be my people."

Ephesians 5:3-4

But among you there must not be even a hint of sexual immorality, or of any kind of impurity, or of greed, because these are improper for God's holy people. Nor should there be obscenity, foolish talk or coarse joking, which are out of place, but rather thanksgiving.

1 Thessalonians 4:3-8

It is God's will that you should be sanctified: that you should avoid sexual immorality; that each of you should learn to control his own body in a way that is holy and hon-orable, not in passionate lust like the heathen, who do not know God; and that in this matter no one should wrong his brother or take advantage of him. The Lord will punish men for all such sins, as we have already told you and warned you. For God did not call us to be impure, but to live a holy life. Therefore, he who rejects this instruction does not reject man but God, who gives you his Holy Spirit.

Hebrews 12:16

See that no one is sexually immoral, or is godless like Esau, who for a single meal sold his inheritance rights as the oldest son.

Hebrews 13:4

Marriage should be honored by all, and the marriage bed kept pure, for God will judge the adulterer and all the sexually immoral.

·· Marriage: Purpose and Beauty of Sex ················

Genesis 2:22-24

Then the LORD God made a woman from the rib he had taken out of the man, and he brought her to the man.
The man said,

"This is now bone of my bones
and flesh of my flesh;
she shall be called 'woman,'
for she was taken out of man."

For this reason a man will leave his father and mother and be united to his wife, and they will become one flesh.

Proverbs 5:15-19

Drink water from your own cistern,
running water from your own well.
Should your springs overflow in the streets,
your streams of water in the public squares?
Let them be yours alone,
never to be shared with strangers.
May your fountain be blessed,
and may you rejoice in the wife of your youth.
A loving doe, a graceful deer—
may her breasts satisfy you always,
may you ever be captivated by her love.

Proverbs 18:22

He who finds a wife finds what is good
and receives favor from the LORD.

Ecclesiastes 9:9

Enjoy life with your wife, whom you love, all the days of this meaningless life that God has given you under the sun—all your meaningless days. For this is your lot in life and in your toilsome labor under the sun.

Mark 10:6-9

"But at the beginning of creation God 'made them male and female.' 'For this reason a man will leave his father and mother and be united to his wife, and the two will become one flesh.' So they are no longer two, but one. Therefore what God has joined together, let man not separate."

 (Illustration: Song of Solomon 4:1-7—Praise of the lover)

··Marriage: Responsibility of Husbands ··················

Ephesians 5:28-33

In this same way, husbands ought to love their wives as their own bodies. He who loves his wife loves himself. After all, no one ever hated his own body, but he feeds and cares for it, just as Christ does the church—for we are members of his body. "For this reason a man will leave his father and mother and be united to his wife, and the two will become one flesh." This is a profound mystery—but I am talking about Christ and the church. However, each one of you also must love his wife as he loves himself, and the wife must respect her husband.

Colossians 3:19

Husbands, love your wives and do not be harsh with them.

1 Peter 3:7

Husbands, in the same way be considerate as you live with your wives, and treat them with respect as the weaker partner and as heirs with you of the gracious gift of life, so that nothing will hinder your prayers.

··Marriage: Responsibility of Wives ·····················

Proverbs 12:4

A wife of noble character is her husband's crown,
    but a disgraceful wife is like decay in his bones.

Ephesians 5:22-24

Wives, submit to your husbands as to the Lord. For the husband is the head of the wife as Christ is the head of the church, his body, of which he is the Savior. Now as the church submits to Christ, so also wives should submit to their husbands in everything.

Ephesians 5:33

However, each one of you also must love his wife as he loves himself, and the wife must respect her husband.

Colossians 3:18

Wives, submit to your husbands, as is fitting in the Lord.

Titus 2:4-5

Then they can train the younger women to love their husbands and children, to be self-controlled and pure, to be busy at home, to be kind, and to be subject to their husbands, so that no one will malign the word of God.

1 Peter 3:1-6

Wives, in the same way be submissive to your husbands so that, if any of them do not believe the word, they may be won over without words by the behavior of their wives, when they see the purity and reverence of your lives. Your beauty should not come from outward adornment, such as braided hair and the wearing of gold jewelry and fine clothes. Instead, it should be that of your inner self, the unfading beauty of a gentle and quiet spirit, which is of great worth in God's sight. For this is the way the holy women of the past who put their hope in God used to make themselves beautiful. They were submissive to their own husbands, like Sarah, who obeyed Abraham and called him her master. You are her daughters if you do what is right and do not give way to fear.

 (Illustration: Proverbs 31:10-31—The wife of noble character)

·· Marriage: Separation and Divorce ····················

Matthew 5:31-32

"It has been said, 'Anyone who divorces his wife must give her a certificate of divorce.' But I tell you that anyone who divorces his wife, except for marital unfaithfulness, causes her to become an adulteress, and anyone who marries the divorced woman commits adultery."

Matthew 19:4-6

"Haven't you read," he replied, "that at the beginning the Creator 'made them male and female,' and said, 'For this reason a man will leave his father and mother and be united to his wife, and the two will become one flesh'? So they are no longer two, but one. Therefore what God has joined together, let man not separate."

1 Corinthians 7:10-11

To the married I give this command (not I, but the Lord): A wife must not separate from her husband. But if she does, she must remain unmarried or else be reconciled to her husband. And a husband must not divorce his wife.

chapter

10

Growing in Speech

97

•• Words Are Powerful ••••••••••••••••••••••••••••••••••

Proverbs 10:11

The mouth of the righteous is a fountain of life,
    but violence overwhelms the mouth of the wicked.

Proverbs 10:20-21

The tongue of the righteous is choice silver,
    but the heart of the wicked is of little value.
The lips of the righteous nourish many,
    but fools die for lack of judgment.

Proverbs 11:11-12

Through the blessing of the upright a city is exalted,
    but by the mouth of the wicked it is destroyed.
A man who lacks judgment derides his neighbor,
    but a man of understanding holds his tongue.

Proverbs 12:18

Reckless words pierce like a sword,
    but the tongue of the wise brings healing.

Proverbs 15:2

The tongue of the wise commends knowledge,
    but the mouth of the fool gushes folly.

Proverbs 15:4

The tongue that brings healing is a tree of life,
    but a deceitful tongue crushes the spirit.

Proverbs 17:4

A wicked man listens to evil lips;
    a liar pays attention to a malicious tongue.

Proverbs 18:21

The tongue has the power of life and death,
    and those who love it will eat its fruit.

Proverbs 21:23

He who guards his mouth and his tongue
    keeps himself from calamity.

Proverbs 25:23

As a north wind brings rain,
so a sly tongue brings angry looks.

Ecclesiastes 5:2-3

Do not be quick with your mouth,
do not be hasty in your heart
to utter anything before God.
God is in heaven
and you are on earth,
so let your words be few.
As a dream comes when there are many cares,
so the speech of a fool when there are many words.

James 1:26

If anyone considers himself religious and yet does not keep a tight rein on his tongue, he deceives himself and his religion is worthless.

James 3:6-8

The tongue also is a fire, a world of evil among the parts of the body. It corrupts the whole person, sets the whole course of his life on fire, and is itself set on fire by hell.

All kinds of animals, birds, reptiles and creatures of the sea are being tamed and have been tamed by man, but no man can tame the tongue. It is a restless evil, full of deadly poison.

1 Peter 3:10

..."Whoever would love life
and see good days
must keep his tongue from evil
and his lips from deceitful speech."

·· Words Can Help: Encouraging Others ················

Proverbs 15:23

A man finds joy in giving an apt reply—
and how good is a timely word!

Proverbs 16:24

Pleasant words are a honeycomb,
sweet to the soul and healing to the bones.

Proverbs 22:11

He who loves a pure heart and whose speech is gracious
will have the king for his friend.

Proverbs 25:11

> A word aptly spoken
> is like apples of gold in settings of silver.

Colossians 4:6

> Let your conversation be always full of grace, seasoned with salt, so that you may know how to answer everyone.

1 Thessalonians 5:11

> Therefore encourage one another and build each other up, just as in fact you are doing.

••Words Can Help: Keeping Promises ••••••••••••••••••••

Numbers 30:2

> When a man makes a vow to the LORD or takes an oath to obligate himself by a pledge, he must not break his word but must do everything he said.

Proverbs 20:25

> It is a trap for a man to dedicate something rashly
> and only later to consider his vows.

Ecclesiastes 5:4

> When you make a vow to God, do not delay in fulfilling it. He has no pleasure in fools; fulfill your vow.

Ecclesiastes 5:5

> It is better not to vow than to make a vow and not fulfill it.

Matthew 5:36-37

> "And do not swear by your head, for you cannot make even one hair white or black. Simply let your 'Yes' be 'Yes,' and your 'No,' 'No'; anything beyond this comes from the evil one."

James 5:12

> Above all, my brothers, do not swear—not by heaven or by earth or by anything else. Let your "Yes" be yes, and your "No," no, or you will be condemned.

••Words Can Help: Keeping Secrets ••••••••••••••••••••

Proverbs 11:13

> A gossip betrays a confidence,
> but a trustworthy man keeps a secret.

Proverbs 20:19

A gossip betrays a confidence;
so avoid a man who talks too much.

Proverbs 25:9-10

If you argue your case with a neighbor,
do not betray another man's confidence,
or he who hears it may shame you
and you will never lose your bad reputation.

Ecclesiastes 10:20

Do not revile the king even in your thoughts,
or curse the rich in your bedroom,
because a bird of the air may carry your words,
and a bird on the wing may report what you say.

•• Words Can Help: Teaching Others ••••••••••••••••••••

Proverbs 16:21

The wise in heart are called discerning,
and pleasant words promote instruction.

Proverbs 20:15

Gold there is, and rubies in abundance,
but lips that speak knowledge are a rare jewel.

Ecclesiastes 9:17

The quiet words of the wise are more to be heeded
than the shouts of a ruler of fools.

Ecclesiastes 12:11

The words of the wise are like goads, their collected sayings like firmly embedded nails—given by one Shepherd.

Romans 12:7

If it is serving, let him serve; if it is teaching, let him teach...

Colossians 1:28

We proclaim him, admonishing and teaching everyone with all wisdom, so that we may present everyone perfect in Christ.

Titus 2:7-8

In everything set them an example by doing what is good. In your teaching show integrity, seriousness and soundness of speech that cannot be condemned, so that those who oppose you may be ashamed because they have nothing bad to say about us.

••Words Can Hurt: Angry Outbursts ••••••••••••••••••••

Proverbs 13:3

> He who guards his lips guards his life,
> but he who speaks rashly will come to ruin.

Proverbs 14:3

> A fool's talk brings a rod to his back,
> but the lips of the wise protect them.

Proverbs 18:6

> A fool's lips bring him strife,
> and his mouth invites a beating.

Proverbs 25:23

> As a north wind brings rain,
> so a sly tongue brings angry looks.

••Words Can Hurt: Boasting ••••••••••••••••••••••••

Proverbs 13:7

> One man pretends to be rich, yet has nothing;
> another pretends to be poor, yet has great wealth.

Proverbs 18:2

> A fool finds no pleasure in understanding
> but delights in airing his own opinions.

Proverbs 27:2

> Let another praise you, and not your own mouth;
> someone else, and not your own lips.

Galatians 6:14

> May I never boast except in the cross of our Lord Jesus
> Christ, through which the world has been crucified to me,
> and I to the world.

James 3:5

> Likewise the tongue is a small part of the body, but it
> makes great boasts. Consider what a great forest is set on
> fire by a small spark.

••Words Can Hurt: Complaining ••••••••••••••••••••••

1 Corinthians 10:10

> And do not grumble, as some of them did—and were
> killed by the destroying angel.

Philippians 2:14

Do everything without complaining or arguing.

James 5:9

Don't grumble against each other, brothers, or you will be judged. The Judge is standing at the door!

(Illustration: Exodus 16:1-3—Children of Israel complaining in the desert)

·· Words Can Hurt: Excusing Your Behavior ··············

Exodus 4:10-11

Moses said to the LORD, "O Lord, I have never been eloquent, neither in the past nor since you have spoken to your servant. I am slow of speech and tongue."

The LORD said to him, "Who gave man his mouth? Who makes him deaf or mute? Who gives him sight or makes him blind? Is it not I, the LORD?"

Psalm 36:2

For in his own eyes he flatters himself
too much to detect or hate his sin.

Proverbs 22:13

The sluggard says, "There is a lion outside!"
or, "I will be murdered in the streets!"

Matthew 25:24

"Then the man who had received the one talent came. 'Master,' he said, 'I knew that you are a hard man, harvesting where you have not sown and gathering where you have not scattered seed.'"

John 15:22

"If I had not come and spoken to them, they would not be guilty of sin. Now, however, they have no excuse for their sin."

Romans 1:20

For since the creation of the world God's invisible qualities—his eternal power and divine nature—have been clearly seen, being understood from what has been made, so that men are without excuse.

(Illustrations: Genesis 3:12-13—Adam and Eve; Luke 14:15-24—The parable of the great banquet)

·· Words Can Hurt: Flattering ······················

Job 32:21
I will show partiality to no one,
nor will I flatter any man.

Proverbs 26:28
A lying tongue hates those it hurts,
and a flattering mouth works ruin.

Proverbs 29:5
Whoever flatters his neighbor
is spreading a net for his feet.

Jude 16
These men are grumblers and faultfinders; they follow
their own evil desires; they boast about themselves and
flatter others for their own advantage.

·· Words Can Hurt: Gossiping ······················

Proverbs 10:18
He who conceals his hatred has lying lips,
and whoever spreads slander is a fool.

Proverbs 11:9
With his mouth the godless destroys his neighbor,
but through knowledge the righteous escape.

Proverbs 11:13
A gossip betrays a confidence,
but a trustworthy man keeps a secret.

Proverbs 16:28
A perverse man stirs up dissension,
and a gossip separates close friends.

Proverbs 17:9
He who covers over an offense promotes love,
but whoever repeats the matter separates close friends.

Proverbs 18:8
The words of a gossip are like choice morsels;
they go down to a man's inmost parts.

Proverbs 26:20
Without wood a fire goes out;
without gossip a quarrel dies down.

James 4:11

Brothers, do not slander one another. Anyone who speaks against his brother or judges him speaks against the law and judges it. When you judge the law, you are not keeping it, but sitting in judgment on it.

•• Words Can Hurt: Lying ••••••••••••••••••••••••••••

Psalm 5:6

You destroy those who tell lies;
bloodthirsty and deceitful men
the LORD abhors.

Proverbs 6:16-19

There are six things the LORD hates,
seven that are detestable to him:
haughty eyes,
a lying tongue,
hands that shed innocent blood,
a heart that devises wicked schemes,
feet that are quick to rush into evil,
a false witness who pours out lies
and a man who stirs up dissension among brothers.

Proverbs 12:19

Truthful lips endure forever,
but a lying tongue lasts only a moment.

Proverbs 12:22

The LORD detests lying lips,
but he delights in men who are truthful.

Proverbs 15:4

The tongue that brings healing is a tree of life,
but a deceitful tongue crushes the spirit.

Proverbs 17:4

A wicked man listens to evil lips;
a liar pays attention to a malicious tongue.

Proverbs 19:9

A false witness will not go unpunished,
and he who pours out lies will perish.

Proverbs 21:6

A fortune made by a lying tongue
is a fleeting vapor and a deadly snare.

Proverbs 25:18

> Like a club or a sword or a sharp arrow
>   is the man who gives false testimony against
>   his neighbor.

Proverbs 26:28

> A lying tongue hates those it hurts,
>   and a flattering mouth works ruin.

John 8:44

> "You belong to your father, the devil, and you want to
> carry out your father's desire. He was a murderer from the
> beginning, not holding to the truth, for there is no truth in
> him. When he lies, he speaks his native language, for he is
> a liar and the father of lies."

Colossians 3:9

> Do not lie to each other, since you have taken off your old
> self with its practices.

Revelation 21:8

> "But the cowardly, the unbelieving, the vile, the murderers,
> the sexually immoral, those who practice magic arts, the
> idolaters and all liars—their place will be in the fiery lake of
> burning sulfur. This is the second death."

·· Words Can Hurt: Mocking ····························

Proverbs 3:34

> He mocks proud mockers
>   but gives grace to the humble.

Proverbs 9:12

> If you are wise, your wisdom will reward you;
>   if you are a mocker, you alone will suffer.

Proverbs 13:1

> A wise son heeds his father's instruction,
>   but a mocker does not listen to rebuke.

Proverbs 14:6

> The mocker seeks wisdom and finds none,
>   but knowledge comes easily to the discerning.

Proverbs 14:9

> Fools mock at making amends for sin,
>   but goodwill is found among the upright.

Proverbs 17:5

He who mocks the poor shows contempt
    for their Maker;
    whoever gloats over disaster will not go unpunished.

Proverbs 21:24

The proud and arrogant man—"Mocker" is his name;
    he behaves with overweening pride.

Proverbs 22:10

Drive out the mocker, and out goes strife;
    quarrels and insults are ended.

Proverbs 24:8-9

He who plots evil
    will be known as a schemer.
The schemes of folly are sin,
    and men detest a mocker.

Proverbs 25:20

Like one who takes away a garment on a cold day,
    or like vinegar poured on soda,
    is one who sings songs to a heavy heart.

Proverbs 29:8

Mockers stir up a city,
    but wise men turn away anger.

Proverbs 30:17

"The eye that mocks a father,
    that scorns obedience to a mother,
will be pecked out by the ravens of the valley,
    will be eaten by the vultures."

Galatians 6:7

Do not be deceived: God cannot be mocked. A man reaps
what he sows.

Hebrews 10:29-31

How much more severely do you think a man deserves to
be punished who has trampled the Son of God under foot,
who has treated as an unholy thing the blood of the
covenant that sanctified him, and who has insulted the
Spirit of grace? For we know him who said, "It is mine to
avenge; I will repay," and again, "The Lord will judge his
people." It is a dreadful thing to fall into the hands of the
living God.

2 Peter 3:3
First of all, you must understand that in the last days scoffers will come, scoffing and following their own evil desires.

··Words Can Hurt: Swearing and Insulting ···············

Proverbs 4:24
Put away perversity from your mouth;
    keep corrupt talk far from your lips.

Proverbs 12:18a
Reckless words pierce like a sword...

Proverbs 15:1-2
A gentle answer turns away wrath,
    but a harsh word stirs up anger.
The tongue of the wise commends knowledge,
    but the mouth of the fool gushes folly.

Matthew 5:22
"But I tell you that anyone who is angry with his brother will be subject to judgment. Again, anyone who says to his brother, 'Raca,' is answerable to the Sanhedrin. But anyone who says, 'You fool!' will be in danger of the fire of hell."

Matthew 12:34-35
"You brood of vipers, how can you who are evil say anything good? For out of the overflow of the heart the mouth speaks. The good man brings good things out of the good stored up in him, and the evil man brings evil things out of the evil stored up in him."

Ephesians 4:29
Do not let any unwholesome talk come out of your mouths, but only what is helpful for building others up according to their needs, that it may benefit those who listen.

··Words Can Hurt: Talking Before Listening ··············

Proverbs 18:13
He who answers before listening—
    that is his folly and his shame.

Proverbs 29:20
Do you see a man who speaks in haste?
    There is more hope for a fool than for him.

Ecclesiastes 5:2
> Do not be quick with your mouth,
>> do not be hasty in your heart
>> to utter anything before God.
> God is in heaven
>> and you are on earth,
>> so let your words be few.

James 1:19
> My dear brothers, take note of this: Everyone should be quick to listen, slow to speak and slow to become angry.

·· Words Can Hurt: Talking Carelessly ···················

Proverbs 10:8
> The wise in heart accept commands,
>> but a chattering fool comes to ruin.

Proverbs 10:10
> He who winks maliciously causes grief,
>> and a chattering fool comes to ruin.

Proverbs 10:19
> When words are many, sin is not absent,
>> but he who holds his tongue is wise.

Proverbs 17:28
> Even a fool is thought wise if he keeps silent,
>> and discerning if he holds his tongue.

Proverbs 18:2
> A fool finds no pleasure in understanding
>> but delights in airing his own opinions.

Proverbs 21:23
> He who guards his mouth and his tongue
>> keeps himself from calamity.

Ecclesiastes 5:3
> As a dream comes when there are many cares,
>> so the speech of a fool when there are many words.

Matthew 12:36
> "But I tell you that men will have to give account on the day of judgment for every careless word they have spoken."

2 Timothy 2:16

Avoid godless chatter, because those who indulge in it will become more and more ungodly.

James 1:26

If anyone considers himself religious and yet does not keep a tight rein on his tongue, he deceives himself and his religion is worthless.

chapter

11

Growing in Spirit

•• Your Awareness of God: God's Care •••••••••••••••••••

Psalm 33:18

But the eyes of the LORD are on those who fear him,
   on those whose hope is in his unfailing love.

Psalm 55:16-18

But I call to God,
   and the LORD saves me.
Evening, morning and noon
   I cry out in distress,
   and he hears my voice.
He ransoms me unharmed
   from the battle waged against me,
   even though many oppose me.

Psalm 55:22

Cast your cares on the LORD
   and he will sustain you;
   he will never let the righteous fall.

Psalm 139:13-15a

For you created my inmost being;
   you knit me together in my mother's womb.
I praise you because I am fearfully
      and wonderfully made;
   your works are wonderful,
   I know that full well.
My frame was not hidden from you
   when I was made in the secret place.

Nahum 1:7

The LORD is good,
   a refuge in times of trouble.
He cares for those who trust in him.

Matthew 10:29-31

"Are not two sparrows sold for a penny? Yet not one of
them will fall to the ground apart from the will of your

Father. And even the very hairs of your head are all numbered. So don't be afraid; you are worth more than many sparrows."

Hebrews 13:5-6

Keep your lives free from the love of money and be content with what you have, because God has said,

"Never will I leave you;
never will I forsake you."

So we say with confidence,

"The Lord is my helper; I will not be afraid.
What can man do to me?"

1 Peter 5:6-7

Humble yourselves, therefore, under God's mighty hand, that he may lift you up in due time. Cast all your anxiety on him because he cares for you.

·· Your Awareness of God: God's Control ···············

Proverbs 16:9

In his heart a man plans his course,
but the LORD determines his steps.

Proverbs 19:21

Many are the plans in a man's heart,
but it is the LORD's purpose that prevails.

Proverbs 21:30-31

There is no wisdom, no insight, no plan
that can succeed against the LORD.
The horse is made ready for the day of battle,
but victory rests with the LORD.

Ecclesiastes 3:11

He has made everything beautiful in its time. He has also set eternity in the hearts of men; yet they cannot fathom what God has done from beginning to end.

Ecclesiastes 3:14-15

I know that everything God does will endure forever; nothing can be added to it and nothing taken from it. God does it so that men will revere him.
Whatever is has already been,
and what will be has been before;
and God will call the past to account.

Matthew 10:28-31

"Do not be afraid of those who kill the body but cannot kill the soul. Rather, be afraid of the One who can destroy both soul and body in hell. Are not two sparrows sold for a penny? Yet not one of them will fall to the ground apart from the will of your Father. And even the very hairs of your head are all numbered. So don't be afraid; you are worth more than many sparrows."

Acts 17:24-27

"The God who made the world and everything in it is the Lord of heaven and earth and does not live in temples built by hands. And he is not served by human hands, as if he needed anything, because he himself gives all men life and breath and everything else. From one man he made every nation of men, that they should inhabit the whole earth; and he determined the times set for them and the exact places where they should live. God did this so that men would seek him and perhaps reach out for him and find him, though he is not far from each one of us."

2 Corinthians 9:8

And God is able to make all grace abound to you, so that in all things at all times, having all that you need, you will abound in every good work.

James 4:13-15

Now listen, you who say, "Today or tomorrow we will go to this or that city, spend a year there, carry on business and make money." Why, you do not even know what will happen tomorrow. What is your life? You are a mist that appears for a little while and then vanishes. Instead, you ought to say, "If it is the Lord's will, we will live and do this or that."

•• Your Awareness of God: God's Discipline ••••••••••••••

Job 5:17-18

"Blessed is the man whom God corrects;
so do not despise the discipline of the Almighty.
For he wounds, but he also binds up;
he injures, but his hands also heal."

Proverbs 3:11-12

My son, do not despise the LORD's discipline
and do not resent his rebuke,

because the LORD disciplines those he loves,
as a father the son he delights in.

Hebrews 12:5-6

And you have forgotten that word of encouragement
that addresses you as sons:

"My son, do not make light of the Lord's discipline,
and do not lose heart when he rebukes you,
because the Lord disciplines those he loves,
and he punishes everyone he accepts as a son."

•• Your Awareness of God: God's Forgiveness ••••••••••••

2 Chronicles 7:14

"...if my people, who are called by my name, will humble
themselves and pray and seek my face and turn from their
wicked ways, then will I hear from heaven and will forgive
their sin and will heal their land."

Job 11:6b

"Know this: God has even forgotten some of your sin."

Psalm 130:3-4

If you, O LORD, kept a record of sins,
O LORD, who could stand?
But with you there is forgiveness;
therefore you are feared.

Isaiah 43:25

"I, even I, am he who blots out
your transgressions, for my own sake,
and remembers your sins no more."

Micah 7:18

Who is a God like you,
who pardons sin and forgives the transgression
of the remnant of his inheritance?
You do not stay angry forever
but delight to show mercy.

Romans 5:8

But God demonstrates his own love for us in this: While
we were still sinners, Christ died for us.

1 John 1:9

If we confess our sins, he is faithful and just and will forgive us our sins and purify us from all unrighteousness.

1 John 2:12

I write to you, dear children,
   because your sins have been forgiven on
      account of his name.

 (Illustration: Luke 15:11-24—Parable of the lost son)

·· Your Awareness of God:
God's Knowledge of Every Person ····················

Psalm 33:13-15

From heaven the LORD looks down
   and sees all mankind;
from his dwelling place he watches
   all who live on earth—
he who forms the hearts of all,
   who considers everything they do.

Psalm 33:18

But the eyes of the LORD are on those who fear him,
   on those whose hope is in his unfailing love.

Proverbs 5:21-22

For a man's ways are in full view of the LORD,
   and he examines all his paths.
The evil deeds of a wicked man ensnare him;
   the cords of his sin hold him fast.

Proverbs 15:3

The eyes of the LORD are everywhere,
   keeping watch on the wicked and the good.

Proverbs 24:12

If you say, "But we knew nothing about this,"
   does not he who weighs the heart perceive it?
Does not he who guards your life know it?
   Will he not repay each person according to what he
      has done?

Matthew 6:3-4

"But when you give to the needy, do not let your left hand
know what your right hand is doing, so that your giving
may be in secret. Then your Father, who sees what is done
in secret, will reward you."

Hebrews 4:13

Nothing in all creation is hidden from God's sight. Everything is uncovered and laid bare before the eyes of him to whom we must give account.

•• Your Awareness of God: God's Plan ••••••••••••••••

1 Corinthians 13:11

When I was a child, I talked like a child, I thought like a child, I reasoned like a child. When I became a man, I put childish ways behind me.

2 Corinthians 5:21

God made him who had no sin to be sin for us, so that in him we might become the righteousness of God.

Ephesians 2:10

For we are God's workmanship, created in Christ Jesus to do good works, which God prepared in advance for us to do.

Philippians 3:12

Not that I have already obtained all this, or have already been made perfect, but I press on to take hold of that for which Christ Jesus took hold of me.

1 Thessalonians 5:16-18

Be joyful always; pray continually; give thanks in all circumstances, for this is God's will for you in Christ Jesus.

James 1:4

Perseverance must finish its work so that you may be mature and complete, not lacking anything.

•• Your Response to God: Bible Study ••••••••••••••••••

Psalm 119:11

I have hidden your word in my heart
   that I might not sin against you.

Psalm 119:98-99

Your commands make me wiser than my enemies,
   for they are ever with me.
I have more insight than all my teachers,
   for I meditate on your statutes.

Acts 17:11

Now the Bereans were of more noble character than the Thessalonians, for they received the message with great eagerness and examined the Scriptures every day to see if what Paul said was true.

Colossians 3:16

Let the word of Christ dwell in you richly as you teach and admonish one another with all wisdom, and as you sing psalms, hymns and spiritual songs with gratitude in your hearts to God.

2 Timothy 3:16

All Scripture is God-breathed and is useful for teaching, rebuking, correcting and training in righteousness.

•• Your Response to God: Commitment •••••••••••••••••••

Deuteronomy 11:1

Love the LORD your God and keep his requirements, his decrees, his laws and his commands always.

2 Chronicles 16:9a

"For the eyes of the LORD range throughout the earth to strengthen those whose hearts are fully committed to him."

Job 11:13-15

"Yet if you devote your heart to him
and stretch out your hands to him,
if you put away the sin that is in your hand
and allow no evil to dwell in your tent,
then you will lift up your face without shame;
you will stand firm and without fear."

Proverbs 16:3

Commit to the LORD whatever you do,
and your plans will succeed.

Proverbs 16:20

Whoever gives heed to instruction prospers,
and blessed is he who trusts in the LORD.

Ecclesiastes 12:1

Remember your Creator
in the days of your youth,
before the days of trouble come

and the years approach when you will say,
"I find no pleasure in them."

Ecclesiastes 12:13-14

Now all has been heard;
  here is the conclusion of the matter:
Fear God and keep his commandments,
  for this is the whole duty of man.
For God will bring every deed into judgment,
  including every hidden thing,
  whether it is good or evil.

Matthew 5:20

"For I tell you that unless your righteousness surpasses that of the Pharisees and the teachers of the law, you will certainly not enter the kingdom of heaven."

Matthew 10:37

"Anyone who loves his father or mother more than me is not worthy of me; anyone who loves his son or daughter more than me is not worthy of me."

John 14:21

"Whoever has my commands and obeys them, he is the one who loves me. He who loves me will be loved by my Father, and I too will love him and show myself to him."

Acts 5:29

Peter and the other apostles replied: "We must obey God rather than men!"

Acts 21:13

Then Paul answered, "Why are you weeping and breaking my heart? I am ready not only to be bound, but also to die in Jerusalem for the name of the Lord Jesus."

Romans 2:13

For it is not those who hear the law who are righteous in God's sight, but it is those who obey the law who will be declared righteous.

·· Your Response to God: Confessing Your Sins ···········

Numbers 5:6-7a

"Say to the Israelites: 'When a man or woman wrongs another in any way and so is unfaithful to the LORD, that person is guilty and must confess the sin he has committed.'"

Psalm 32:5

Then I acknowledged my sin to you
    and did not cover up my iniquity.
I said, "I will confess
    my transgressions to the LORD"—
and you forgave
    the guilt of my sin.

Psalm 38:18

I confess my iniquity;
    I am troubled by my sin.

Proverbs 28:13

He who conceals his sins does not prosper,
    but whoever confesses and renounces them finds
mercy.

Mark 1:5

The whole Judean countryside and all the people of Jerusalem went out to him. Confessing their sins, they were baptized by him in the Jordan River.

James 5:16

Therefore confess your sins to each other and pray for each other so that you may be healed. The prayer of a righteous man is powerful and effective.

1 John 1:9

If we confess our sins, he is faithful and just and will forgive us our sins and purify us from all unrighteousness.

•• Your Response to God: Discipleship ••••••••••••••••••

Mark 1:17-18

"Come follow me," Jesus said, "and I will make you fishers of men." At once they left their nets and followed him.

Luke 14:33

"In the same way, any of you who does not give up everything he has cannot be my disciple."

John 8:31-32

To the Jews who had believed him, Jesus said, "If you hold to my teaching, you are really my disciples. Then you will know the truth, and the truth will set you free."

John 13:34-35

"A new command I give you: Love one another. As I have loved you, so you must love one another. By this all men will know that you are my disciples, if you love one another."

John 15:8

"This is to my Father's glory, that you bear much fruit, showing yourselves to be my disciples."

Hebrews 6:12b

...imitate those who through faith and patience inherit what has been promised.

1 John 2:6

Whoever claims to live in him must walk as Jesus did.

··Your Response to God: Fruitfulness ···················

Proverbs 11:30

The fruit of the righteous is a tree of life,
   and he who wins souls is wise.

Matthew 28:19-20

"Therefore go and make disciples of all nations, baptizing them in the name of the Father and of the Son and of the Holy Spirit, and teaching them to obey everything I have commanded you. And surely I am with you always, to the very end of the age."

John 15:16

"You did not choose me, but I chose you and appointed you to go and bear fruit—fruit that will last. Then the Father will give you whatever you ask in my name."

Galatians 5:22-26

But the fruit of the Spirit is love, joy, peace, patience, kindness, goodness, faithfulness, gentleness and self-control. Against such things there is no law. Those who belong to Christ Jesus have crucified the sinful nature with its passions and desires. Since we live by the Spirit, let us keep in step with the Spirit. Let us not become conceited, provoking and envying each other.

Colossians 1:10

And we pray this in order that you may live a life worthy of the Lord and may please him in every way: bearing fruit in every good work, growing in the knowledge of God.

•• Your Response to God: Group Worship (Church Attendance) ••••••••••••••••••••••••••••••

Psalm 100

Shout for joy to the LORD, all the earth.
Worship the LORD with gladness;
come before him with joyful songs.
Know that the LORD is God.
It is he who made us, and we are his;
we are his people, the sheep of his pasture.
Enter his gates with thanksgiving
and his courts with praise;
give thanks to him and praise his name.
For the LORD is good and his love endures forever;
his faithfulness continues through all generations.

Matthew 18:20

"For where two or three come together in my name, there am I with them."

Acts 2:46a

Every day they continued to meet together in the temple courts.

Acts 14:27

On arriving there, they gathered the church together and reported all that God had done through them and how he had opened the door of faith to the Gentiles.

Acts 16:13

On the Sabbath we went outside the city gate to the river, where we expected to find a place of prayer. We sat down and began to speak to the women who had gathered there.

Hebrews 10:25

Let us not give up meeting together, as some are in the habit of doing, but let us encourage one another—and all the more as you see the Day approaching.

•• Your Response to God: Membership in the Body ••••••••

Romans 12:5

So in Christ, we who are many form one body, and each member belongs to all the others.

1 Corinthians 12:12

The body is a unit, though it is made up of many parts; and though all its parts are many, they form one body. So it is with Christ.

1 Corinthians 12:18-20

But in fact God has arranged the parts in the body every one of them, just as he wanted them to be. If they were all one part where would the body be? As it is, there are many parts, but one body.

1 Corinthians 12:27

Now you are the body of Christ, and each one of you is a part of it.

Ephesians 4:3-5

Make every effort to keep the unity of the Spirit through the bond of peace. There is one body and one Spirit—just as you were called to one hope when you were called—one Lord, one faith, one baptism; one God and Father of all, who is over all and through all and in all.

Ephesians 4:15-16

Instead, speaking the truth in love, we will in all things grow up into him who is the Head, that is, Christ. From him the whole body, joined and held together by every supporting ligament, grows and builds itself up in love, as each part does its work.

Ephesians 4:25

Therefore, each of you must put off falsehood and speak truthfully to his neighbor, for we are all members of one body.

Colossians 1:18a

And he is the head of the body, the church.

·· Your Response to God: Personal Faith ················

Proverbs 30:5

"Every word of God is flawless;
  he is a shield to those who take refuge in him."

Ezekiel 18:20

The soul who sins is the one who will die. The son will not share the guilt of the father, nor will the father share the guilt of the son. The righteousness of the righteous man will be credited to him, and the wickedness of the wicked will be charged against him.

Mark 16:16

"Whoever believes and is baptized will be saved, but whoever does not believe will be condemned."

John 11:25-27

Jesus said to her, "I am the resurrection and the life. He who believes in me will live, even though he dies; and whoever lives and believes in me will never die. Do you believe this?"

"Yes, Lord," she told him, "I believe that you are the Christ, the Son of God, who was to come into the world."

Romans 10:9-10

That if you confess with your mouth, "Jesus is Lord," and believe in your heart that God raised him from the dead, you will be saved. For it is with your heart that you believe and are justified, and it is with your mouth that you confess and are saved.

Galatians 5:6

For in Christ Jesus neither circumcision nor uncircumcision has any value. The only thing that counts is faith expressing itself through love.

Hebrews 11:1

Now faith is being sure of what we hope for and certain of what we do not see.

Hebrews 13:15

Through Jesus, therefore, let us continually offer to God a sacrifice of praise—the fruit of lips that confess his name.

·· Your Response to God: Prayer ····················

Mark 11:24

"Therefore I tell you, whatever you ask for in prayer, believe that you have received it, and it will be yours."

Luke 6:28b

"Pray for those who mistreat you."

1 Thessalonians 5:17

Pray continually.

James 4:3
> When you ask, you do not receive, because you ask with wrong motives, that you may spend what you get on your pleasures.

James 5:13
> Is any one of you in trouble? He should pray. Is anyone happy? Let him sing songs of praise.

 (Illustration: Luke 18:2-8—Parable of the persistent widow)

·· Your Response to God: Respect for God (Fear of God) ··

1 Samuel 12:24
> But be sure to fear the LORD and serve him faithfully with all your heart; consider what great things he has done for you.

Proverbs 1:7
> The fear of the LORD is the beginning of knowledge,
>   but fools despise wisdom and discipline.

Proverbs 3:7-8
> Do not be wise in your own eyes;
>   fear the LORD and shun evil.
> This will bring health to your body
>   and nourishment to your bones.

Proverbs 10:27
> The fear of the LORD adds length to life,
>   but the years of the wicked are cut short.

Proverbs 14:2
> He whose walk is upright fears the LORD,
>   but he whose ways are devious despises him.

Proverbs 15:16
> Better a little with the fear of the LORD
>   than great wealth with turmoil.

Proverbs 15:33
> The fear of the LORD teaches a man wisdom,
>   and humility comes before honor.

Proverbs 22:4
> Humility and the fear of the LORD
>   bring wealth and honor and life.

Proverbs 23:17-18

Do not let your heart envy sinners,
>   but always be zealous for the fear of the LORD.
There is surely a future hope for you,
>   and your hope will not be cut off.

Proverbs 28:14

Blessed is the man who always fears the LORD,
>   but he who hardens his heart falls into trouble.

Proverbs 31:30

Charm is deceptive, and beauty is fleeting;
>   but a woman who fears the LORD is to be praised.

Ecclesiastes 12:13

Now all has been heard;
>   here is the conclusion of the matter:
Fear God and keep his commandments,
>   for this is the whole duty of man.

Matthew 10:28

"Do not be afraid of those who kill the body but cannot kill the soul. Rather, be afraid of the One who can destroy both soul and body in hell."

Revelation 14:7

He said in a loud voice, "Fear God and give him glory, because the hour of his judgment has come. Worship him who made the heavens, the earth, the sea and the springs of water."

 (Illustration: Acts 10:1-8—Cornelius, a God-fearing man)

·· Your Response to God: Righteousness ···················

Psalm 37:25-26

I was young and now I am old,
>   yet I have never seen the righteous forsaken
>   or their children begging bread.
They are always generous and lend freely;
>   their children will be blessed.

Proverbs 10:28

The prospect of the righteous is joy,
>   but the hopes of the wicked come to nothing.

Proverbs 11:5

The righteousness of the blameless makes a straight way
for them,
but the wicked are brought down by their
own wickedness.

Proverbs 11:31

If the righteous receive their due on earth,
how much more the ungodly and the sinner!

Proverbs 12:21

No harm befalls the righteous,
but the wicked have their fill of trouble.

Proverbs 13:5-6

The righteous hate what is false,
but the wicked bring shame and disgrace.
Righteousness guards the man of integrity,
but wickedness overthrows the sinner.

Proverbs 13:9

The light of the righteous shines brightly,
but the lamp of the wicked is snuffed out.

Proverbs 24:15-16

Do not lie in wait like an outlaw against a righteous
man's house,
do not raid his dwelling place;
for though a righteous man falls seven times,
he rises again,
but the wicked are brought down by calamity.

•• Your Response to God: Sharing Your Faith ••••••••••••

Psalm 89:15-16a

Blessed are those who have learned to acclaim you,
who walk in the light of your presence, O LORD.
They rejoice in your name all day long."

Isaiah 6:8

Then I heard the voice of the Lord saying, "Whom shall I
send? And who will go for us?"
And I said, "Here am I. Send me!"

Jeremiah 1:4–8

The word of the LORD came to me, saying,

"Before I formed you in the womb I knew you,
before you were born, I set you apart;
I appointed you as a prophet to the nations."

"Ah, Sovereign LORD," I said, "I do not know how to speak;
I am only a child."

But the LORD said to me, "Do not say, 'I am only a child.'
You must go to everyone I send you to and say whatever
I command you. Do not be afraid of them, for I am with
you and will rescue you," declares the LORD.

Matthew 28:18–19a

Then Jesus came to them and said, "All authority in heav-
en and on earth has been given to me. Therefore go and
make disciples of all nations..."

Philemon 6

I pray that you may be active in sharing your faith, so that
you will have a full understanding of every good thing we
have in Christ.

·· Your Response to God: Trust in God ················

Psalm 37:3–9

Trust in the LORD and do good;
dwell in the land and enjoy safe pasture.
Delight yourself in the LORD
and he will give you the desires of your heart.
Commit your way to the LORD;
trust in him and he will do this:
He will make your righteousness shine like the dawn,
the justice of your cause like the noonday sun.
Be still before the LORD and wait patiently for him;
do not fret when men succeed in their ways,
when they carry out their wicked schemes.
Refrain from anger and turn from wrath;
do not fret—it leads only to evil.
For evil men will be cut off,
but those who hope in the LORD will inherit the land.

Proverbs 3:5

Trust in the LORD with all your heart
and lean not on your own understanding.

Proverbs 11:28

Whoever trusts in his riches will fall,
    but the righteous will thrive like a green leaf.

Proverbs 16:20

Whoever gives heed to instruction prospers,
    and blessed is he who trusts in the LORD.

Proverbs 28:25-26

A greedy man stirs up dissension,
    but he who trusts in the LORD will prosper.
He who trusts in himself is a fool,
    but he who walks in wisdom is kept safe.

Proverbs 29:25

Fear of man will prove to be a snare,
    but whoever trusts in the LORD is kept safe.

chapter

12

Growing in Work Habits

·· Being Dependable ··································

Psalm 37:21
The wicked borrow and do not repay,
    but the righteous give generously.

Matthew 5:37a
"Simply let your 'Yes' be 'Yes,' and your 'No,' 'No.'"

Luke 16:10
"Whoever can be trusted with very little can also be trusted with much, and whoever is dishonest with very little will also be dishonest with much."

 (Illustration: Matthew 21:28-32—Parable of the two sons)

·· Being Motivated by Rewards and Success ··············

Proverbs 12:24
Diligent hands will rule,
    but laziness ends in slave labor.

Proverbs 16:3
Commit to the LORD whatever you do,
    and your plans will succeed.

Proverbs 21:5
The plans of the diligent lead to profit
    as surely as haste leads to poverty.

Proverbs 22:29
Do you see a man skilled in his work?
    He will serve before kings;
    he will not serve before obscure men.

Proverbs 31:27
She watches over the affairs of her household
    and does not eat the bread of idleness.

John 15:16

"You did not choose me, but I chose you and appointed you to go and bear fruit—fruit that will last. Then the Father will give you whatever you ask in my name."

2 Corinthians 8:7

But just as you excel in everything—in faith, in speech, in knowledge, in complete earnestness and in your love for us—see that you also excel in this grace of giving.

Philippians 4:8

Finally, brothers, whatever is true, whatever is noble, whatever is right, whatever is pure, whatever is lovely, whatever is admirable—if anything is excellent or praiseworthy—think about such things.

Colossians 3:23

Whatever you do, work at it with all your heart, as working for the Lord, not for men.

1 Thessalonians 4:11-12

Make it your ambition to lead a quiet life, to mind your own business and to work with your hands, just as we told you, so that your daily life may win the respect of outsiders and so that you will not be dependent on anybody.

Hebrews 6:12

We do not want you to become lazy, but to imitate those who through faith and patience inherit what has been promised.

1 Peter 2:9

But you are a chosen people, a royal priesthood, a holy nation, a people belonging to God, that you may declare the praises of him who called you out of darkness into his wonderful light.

 (Illustration: Matthew 25:14-30—Parable of the talents)

··Laziness ···

Proverbs 15:19

The way of the sluggard is blocked with thorns,
   but the path of the upright is a highway.

Proverbs 18:9
One who is slack in his work
is brother to one who destroys.

Proverbs 19:15
Laziness brings on deep sleep,
and the shiftless man goes hungry.

Proverbs 19:24
The sluggard buries his hand in the dish;
he will not even bring it back to his mouth!

Proverbs 20:4
A sluggard does not plow in season;
so at harvest time he looks but finds nothing.

Proverbs 20:13
Do not love sleep or you will grow poor;
stay awake and you will have food to spare.

Proverbs 21:25-26
The sluggard's craving will be the death of him,
because his hands refuse to work.
All day long he craves for more,
but the righteous give without sparing.

Proverbs 24:30-34
I went past the field of the sluggard,
past the vineyard of the man who lacks judgment;
thorns had come up everywhere,
the ground was covered with weeds,
and the stone wall was in ruins.
I applied my heart to what I observed
and learned a lesson from what I saw:
A little sleep, a little slumber,
a little folding of the hands to rest—
and poverty will come on you like a bandit
and scarcity like an armed man.

Proverbs 26:14
As a door turns on its hinges,
so a sluggard turns on his bed.

Proverbs 26:16
The sluggard is wiser in his own eyes
than seven men who answer discreetly.

Ecclesiastes 10:18
> If a man is lazy, the rafters sag;
>> if his hands are idle, the house leaks.

2 Thessalonians 3:10
> For even when we were with you, we gave you this rule:
> "If a man will not work, he shall not eat."

··Taking Care of Your Pet(s) ·····················

Proverbs 12:10
> A righteous man cares for the needs of his animal,
>> but the kindest acts of the wicked are cruel.

··Taking Care of Your Possessions ·····················

Proverbs 12:27
> The lazy man does not roast his game,
>> but the diligent man prizes his possessions.

Proverbs 21:20
> In the house of the wise are stores of choice
>> food and oil,
> but a foolish man devours all he has.

··Taking Care of Your Room ·····················

Proverbs 14:1
> The wise woman builds her house,
>> but with her own hands the foolish one
>>> tears hers down.

1 Corinthians 14:33a
> For God is not a God of disorder but of peace.

INDEX

Who Are We?

Discipleship Publications International (DPI) began publishing in 1993. We are a nonprofit Christian publisher affiliated with the International Churches of Christ, committed to publishing and distributing materials that honor God, lift up Jesus Christ and show how his message practically applies to all areas of life. We have a deep conviction that no one changes lives like Jesus and that the implementation of his teaching will revolutionize any life, any marriage, any family and any singles household.

Since our beginning, we have published more than 100 titles; plus, we have produced a number of important, spiritual audio products. More than one million volumes have been printed, and our works have been translated into more than a dozen languages—international is not just a part of our name! Our books are shipped regularly to every inhabited continent.

To see a more detailed description of our works, find us on the World Wide Web at www.dpibooks.org. You can order books by calling 1-888-DPI-BOOK twenty-four hours a day. From outside the US, call 781-937-3883, ext. 231 during Boston-area business hours.

We appreciate the hundreds of comments we have received from readers. We would love to hear from you. Here are other ways to get in touch:

Mail: DPI, One Merrill St., Woburn, MA 01801
E-Mail: dpibooks@icoc.org

Find Us on the
World Wide Web

www.dpibooks.org

1-888-DPI-BOOK

outside US: 781-937-3883 x231

Kingdom Kids at Home

Kingdom Kids at Home is an imprint of DPI. Every Kingdom Kids at Home book will be written to help parents who are eager to develop a strong love for God and for Jesus Christ in their children's hearts.

Many influences compete for our children's attention. Every possible tool is needed in the great spiritual battle for their souls. It is our prayer that children everywhere will find the Kingdom Kids at Home books and resources to contain an exciting and stimulating presentation of eternal truths that they will hold to throughout their lives.

DPI considers our partnership with parents to be crucial in this effort. We welcome your feedback and ideas. Please use the e-mail address you find on our web site to give us your thoughts.

We are serious about doing all we can to assist you in passing the gospel on to the next generation.

Continuing to draw from the curriculum and other materials, future books will equip families with tools that they need to water the seeds of faith being planted in their children's hearts.

Currently available (see on following page):

- Three workbooks that mirror the topics covered in the first year of the Kingdom Kids curriculum, including the weekly memory verses. See these books on the top half of the following page.
- Volume One of the *Kingdom Kids Songbook* and CD, which are comprised of the majority of the songs for the first year of the preschool curriculum (and other children's songs).

Other Resources

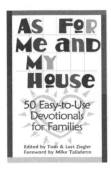

(888) DPI-BOOK

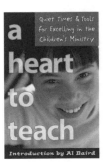